Introduction

Tons of young people love Manga, and it also counts on many fans since the '70s, when the first Japanese cartoons, now called Anime, landed in Italy. Back then, the Manga was still a bit rough and hard to define; nonetheless, it created imprinting of typical shapes and drawings within the hearts of those who were children at the time.

Manga style has become increasingly popular. Fifteen years ago, it was known only by niches. However, in recent years it has become well-known thanks to particular fashions. Today everyone knows more or less what it is.

Manga is a world apart, to all intents and purposes; it is real, and it has well-defined characteristics. These features permit it to claim its own identity, which is not devoid of value, technique, and art. Some school textbooks talk about the spreading of Manga as a new, recognized art form.

Manga drawing could be made correctly or not, and it depends on the study that was done in the first place, as it occurs in many other art forms. Drawing in this style does not disregard the essential notions of drawing, perspective, and volumes. Otherwise, these aspects that give three-dimensionality and professionalism to a drawing would not be able to emerge.

Copying and drawing Manga without studying it can be an initial phase to approach this world and to get familiar with it. However, to move to a real and robust approach, it is appropriate to learn the techniques underlying this style. This manual will provide a step-by-step explanation of a variety of usable exercises at all levels and will lead to harmonious and well-done drawings

INDEX

Introduction 1
Index 3

SECOND SECTION, INKING AND COLORING 5

Second section materials 6

1. Inking the drawing 8

1.1   Inking 8
1.2   Shadow's study 14

2. Fillings 19

2.1   Chiaroscuro 19
2.2   Hatching 20
2.3   Halftoning 24
2.4   Filling effects 30
2.5   Coloring: the pantone 32

Informations and contacts 42

Second section
Inking and coloring

Second section
Materials

Inking tools and fillers.

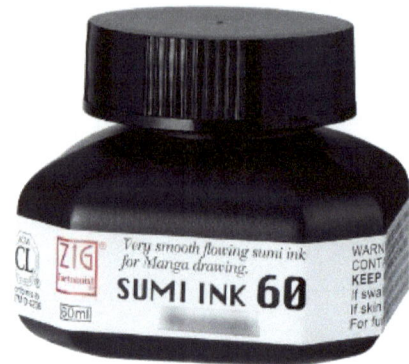
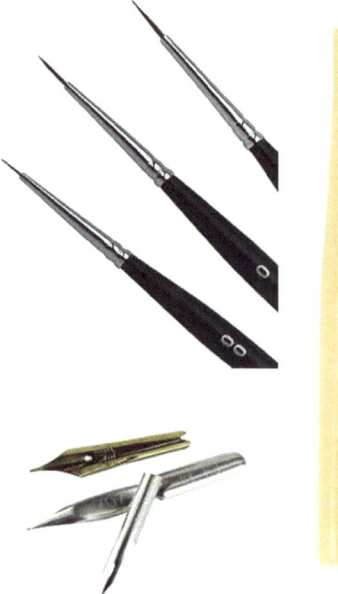

Before starting to ink, you need multiliners, markers, India ink, paintbrushes, and nibs to try the various tools and to choose the most suitable for your hand and style. The nib tips are interchangeable, of different shapes, and hardness. The paintbrushes are much softer, and they should not be too large because their stroke is already variable. In any case, you can decide the final sizes after trying and choosing your preferred style. India ink is excellent ink with a deep black color.

Fude-Pen

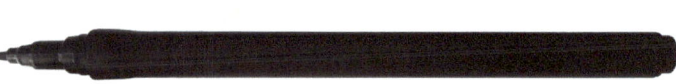

Other tools to choose from are nibs with refillable cartridges and the fude-pen. This rechargeable pen offers similar performance to the paintbrush but is much more practical. It comes in different sizes.

Multiliners

They are ink pens with a synthetic tip, often used for technical drawing.

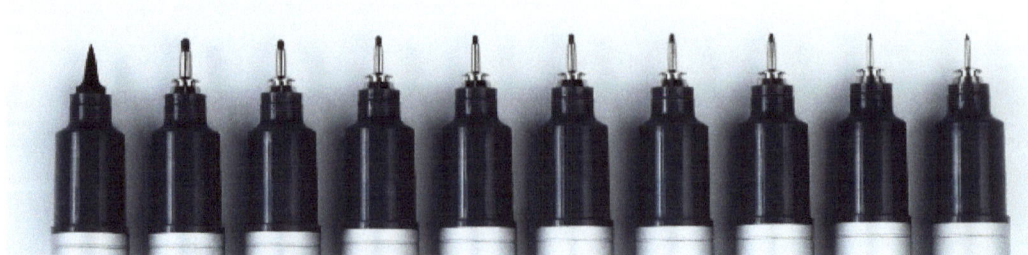

Cutter

It is used to cut and work the halftone screens. The blades are interchangeable, and they came in various shapes, each one is suitable for different processing. For precision works, there are cutters with a ceramic tip.

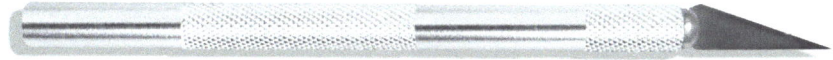

Halftone Screens

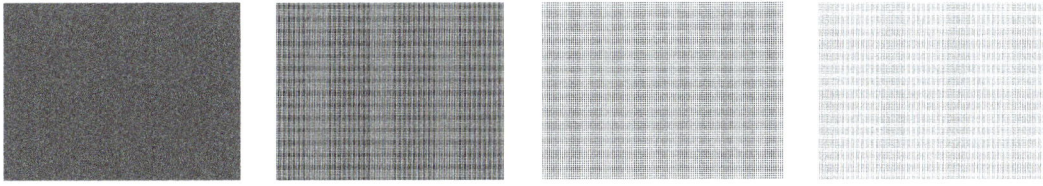

There are many types of halftone screens, but we will talk about the adhesive ones. Even the proposed plots are endless. With the arrival of digital tools, the models have increased exponentially.

The Pantone

It is a felt-tip pen with an ink capable of spreading out to create uniform colors and shades. There are many types of pantone: you can use those with a super-brush tip like a paintbrush.

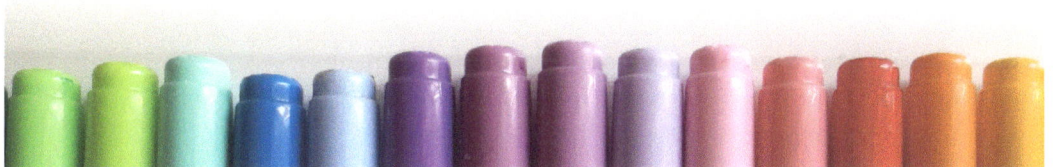

1. Inking the drawing

1.1 Inking

When we talk about inking, we refer to a technique with which we strengthen the outline of the picture and give thickness to the shadows with hatchings or full blacks.

For inking, you can use multiliners, markers, nibs, and paintbrushes.

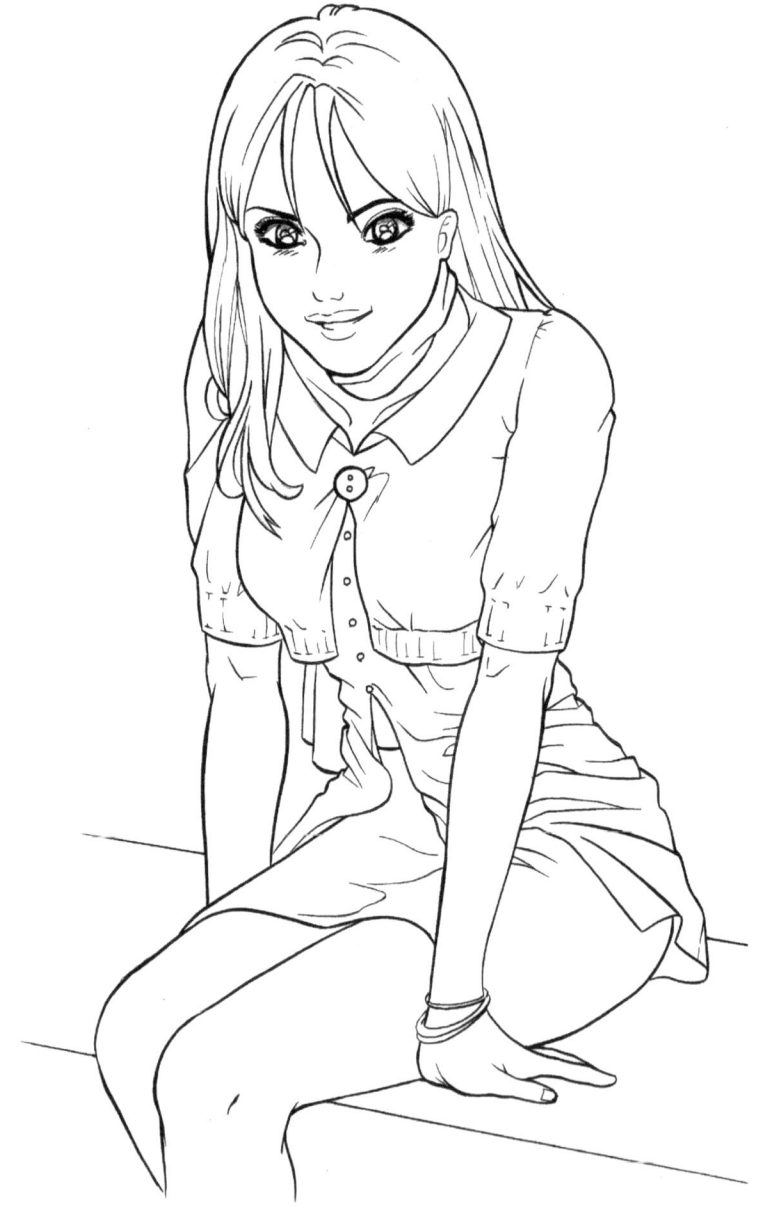

Each of the tools used produces a different stroke, which, together with the artist's hand, characterizes the inking style.

Initially, the tools par excellence were the paintbrush and the nib, which were very ancient and typical of Japanese and Chinese cultures. Over time, many variations developed with the introduction of other inking tools.

There are two macro-categories for inking, and they can coexist in the same drawing: **synthetic** (multiliners and markers), with **India ink** (paintbrushes and nibs).
The difference lies down in two aspects: rendering of the stroke and practicality.

With **multiliners** and **markers**, you have an unmodulated stroke, i.e., it does not change according to pressure. You have to go over it again to thicken the line. The blacks unlikely will be full and brilliant as those of the India ink. However, these tools are efficient because they do not have to be dipped in ink every time.

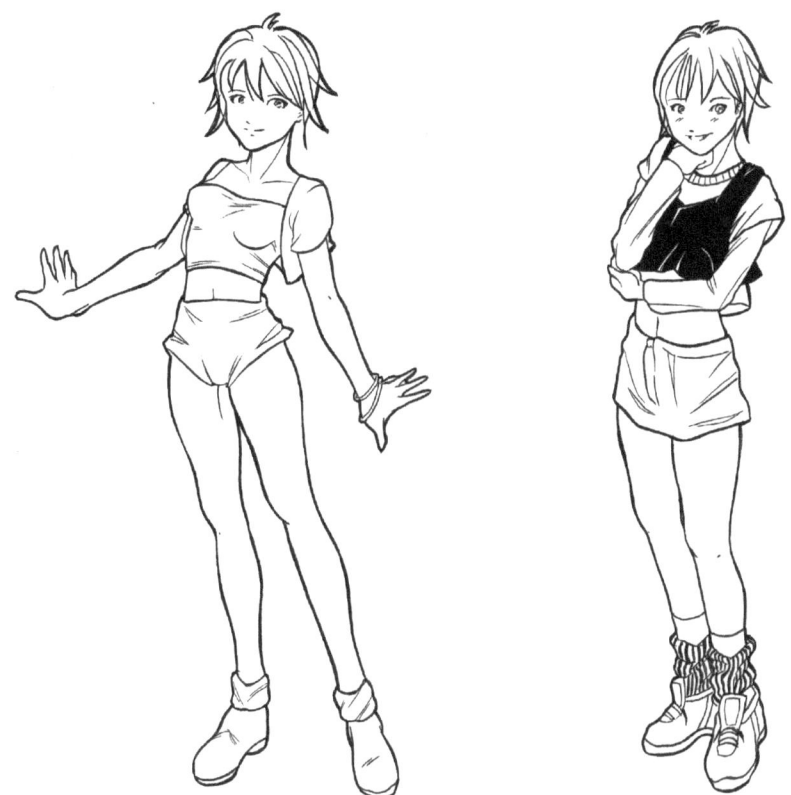

Paintbrushes and **nibs** allow creating strokes that change thickness without interruption, giving harmony and softness to the drawing, with a simple change of pressure. The paintbrush is much more sensitive than the nib, and it also offers chiaroscuro effects. The India ink has intense and brilliant blacks, and the only flaw is that both tools need to be dipped into the ink very often.

A halfway tool between the two categories is the **fude-pen**, a marker pen with a bristle tip. It deserves to be put on the list as it combines the practicality of an ink tank with the characteristic of the soft, modulated stroke of the paintbrush. In Manga, it is used both for inking and for filling backgrounds.

The technique:

As we said, inking involves the contours but also the shadow part. To fill wide **backgrounds** with black, use a wide tip (paintbrush or marker).

For **buildings** and **geometrical objects**, multilines are more practical even if there are less efficient paintbrush/nib ruler techniques.

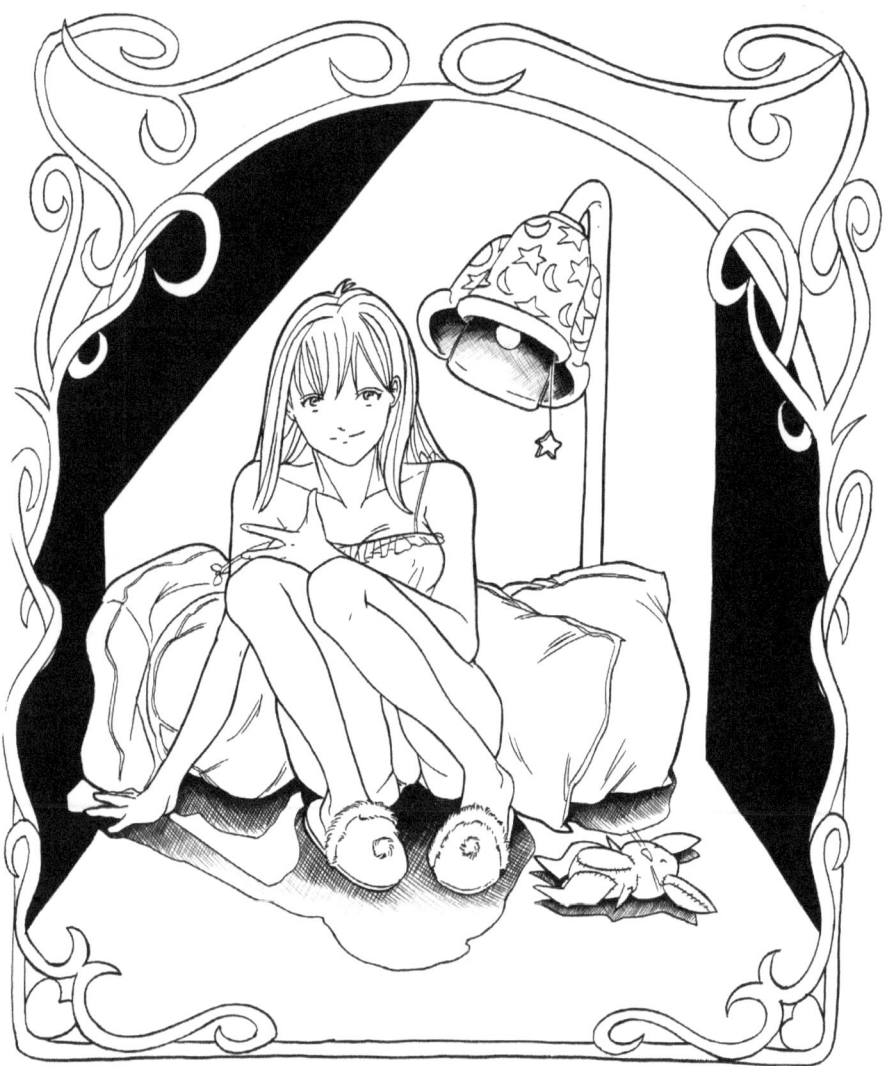

To ink the subjects, choose your favorite tool.

- The paintbrush is undoubtedly the softest and most adjustable (picture above).
- The nib offers a smaller but still valuable and pleasant dynamic stroke. The stroke is a bit stiff, but the nibs can make extremely thin lines.
- Markers are suitable for backgrounds. Multiliners have a nib's similar style, but you cannot modulate the stroke with pressure.

The inking style is very personal. However, some rules can make it perfect if correctly practiced.

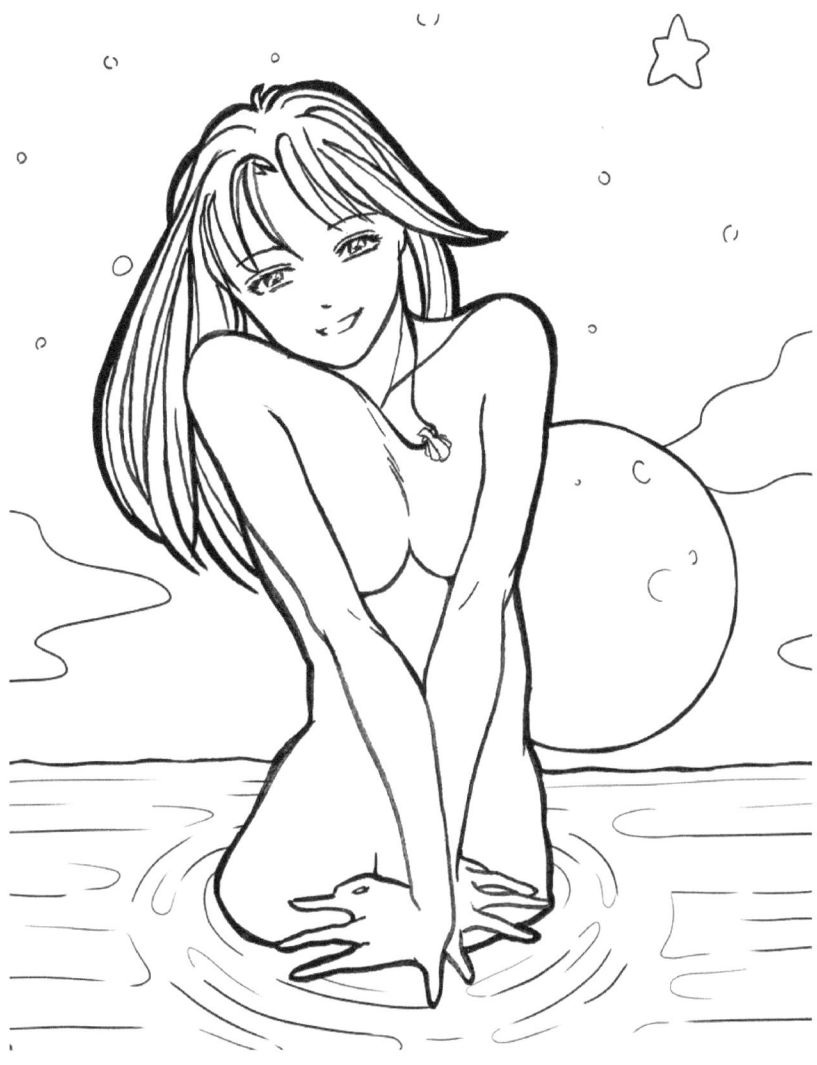

Within the drawing, there are various levels: the closest to the observer and the farthest one. The **distant** backgrounds will be inked with a **thin stroke**, while the figures on the **nearest** level inked with **broader strokes**. To avoid confusion, draw the details with thin lines.

Another technique is to thicken the stroke to **"detach" the levels**.

To give depth to the drawing, consider detaching a figure on a nearby level from another on the plane behind.
This technique is present in characters with a thicker outline, so they emerge from the background. But is also applies to an extreme close up of a hand that has to be detached from the arm behind.

How to ink with paintbrush and nib:

Prepare the India ink, some water, and a sheet. Dilute the India ink with water to reach the desired ink's fluidity suitable for the strokes and, in some cases, could help to create shades of grey. Do not mix water inside the India ink's container, but separately.

After dipping the nib or the paintbrush, **drain** it from ink's surplus. On a test sheet, check the stroke to see if the ink's dilution and its amount on the tip are optimal for your hand and stroke.

Nib

Paintbrush

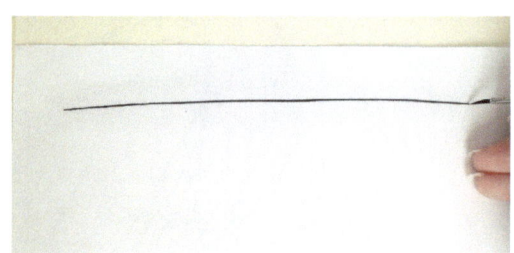

The stroke should be homogeneous without smears, shaking, interruptions, and visible fading of the India ink.

The hand must be firm, and it's advantageous to consider the amount of ink available.

Once the drawing's stroke is defined, the work of inking is only halfway through, because it also consists of another phase relating to shadows, chiaroscuro, and filling in the "black" areas.

You can ink shadows using hatching, halftoning, sponging, or other techniques, including full black filling.

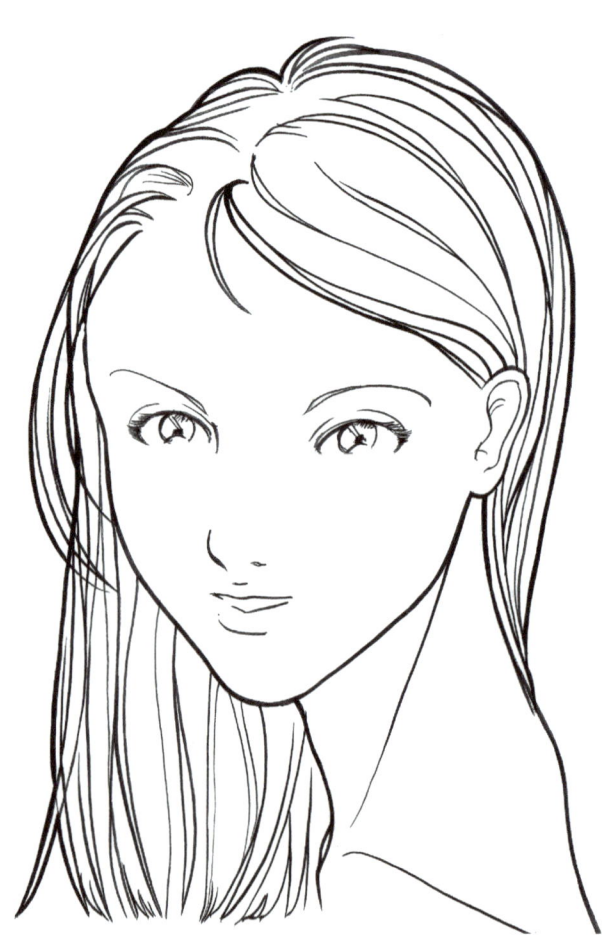

It will take some practice to learn how to balance the hand, the amount of ink, and the dilution. Here are some examples of the most common stroke's mistakes and their causes.

Nib	**Paintbrush**

This is an example of a shaky stroke, a symptom of an insecure hand.

In this case, the ink is excessively diluted; even if the stroke is fluid, the India ink is grey and not covering.

If using the nib you end up with something like that, these could be the causes:
- a little amount of ink on the nib.
- the ink must be diluted.
- you are applying too much pressure on the sheet.

If the stroke resembles the one in the image with the paintbrush, it means that an India ink's dilution is needed. It's necessary to stop inking before the India ink ends to avoid strips.

 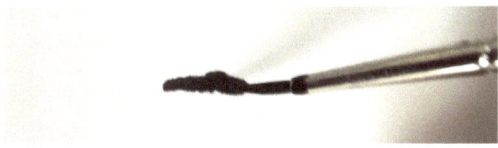

Placing the nib on the sheet of paper may cause stains that could ruin the drawing if you do not drain the India ink's excess from the tip.

The ink will be poured over the sheet if you place the paintbrush just dipped in India ink without discharging the excess. With the paintbrush, this effect is much more frequent than with the nib.

Some very practical exercises to learn how to get a good stroke, consist of repeating equidistant horizontal and vertical lines, and precisely closed circles of various sizes. These exercises allow developing manual skills and controlling the stroke in all its characteristics, including pressure and density.

1.2 Shadow's study

The drawing does not consist only of contours but of **shadow** zones and **light points**. Therefore, it is indispensable to make a study on the subject because without it is difficult to apply any form of filling.

Shadows are generated according to the light's source, the object's material, and the shape of the object itself.

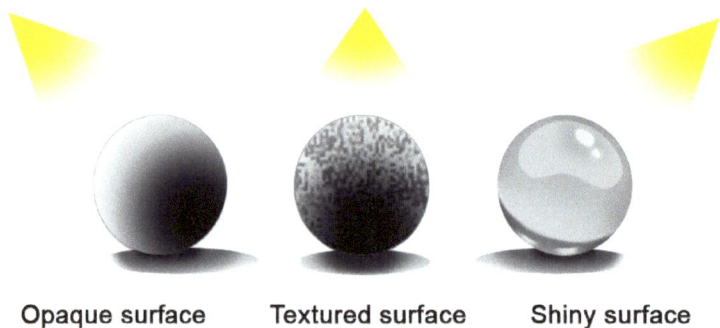

Opaque surface   Textured surface   Shiny surface

This concept explains that **drawing a shadow in the wrong way also changes the shape of the subject.**

Core shadows (the object's shadows) are areas of the object where there is no light.
Cast shadows (e.g., on the ground or a wall) are shadows cast by the object on surfaces.

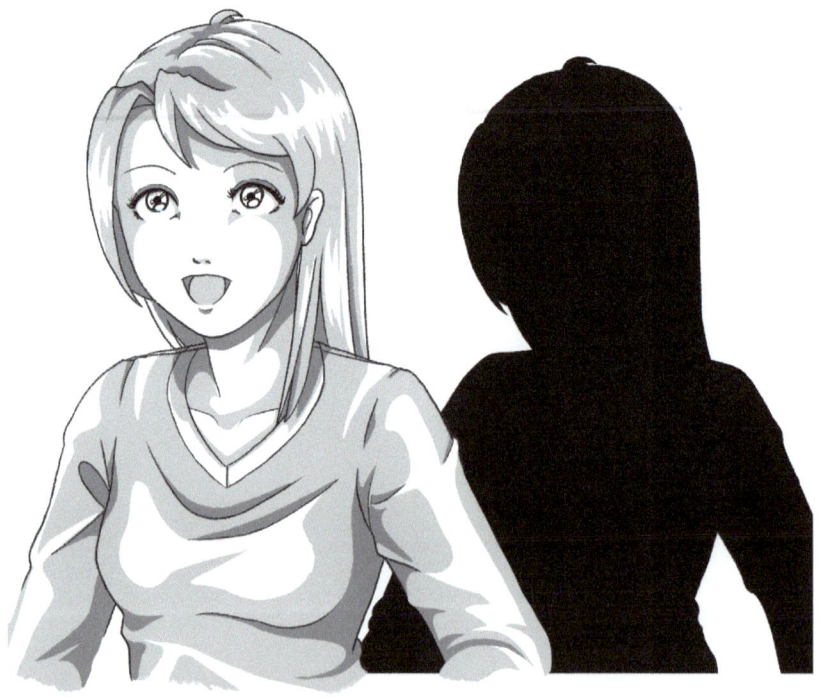

There are 3 elements that give shape and intensity to the shadows:

1) The light source determines the position and depth of the shadows.

If the light cannot reach a place, there is shadow. Therefore, the shadow is located on the opposite side of light's source or in hidden areas. The shadow is **dark** with the sharp outline if what creates the shadow is **near**; it is **fair** and **shaded** if what creates the shadow is **far**.

2) The surface of the object receiving the light can be **shiny, opaque, and irregular with texture** (a sweater, a tree).

If the surface is shiny, the shadows and the light points are sharp and marked (white light, dark shadow).
If the surface is opaque, the shadow is homogeneous and shaded.
In the case of texture, the shadow will be irregular with light and shadow matching the ripples.

3) The shape of the object has the most significant impact on the generation of shadows (and lights).

Let us take a face as an example: a shadow starting from the contour of the face and finishing under the cheekbones, creates the effect of a thin, hollowed-out look. If we draw the shadow only around the face, instead, with soft lines, it will look round.

Likewise, if you draw a large shadow under the nose or sideways, the nose will look larger or longer **because the shadow determines the shape**.

We have to make things right if we want shadows and lights to respect the shapes we have decided to draw.

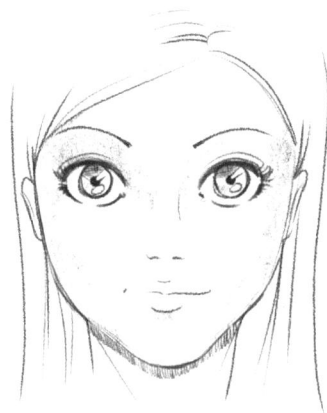
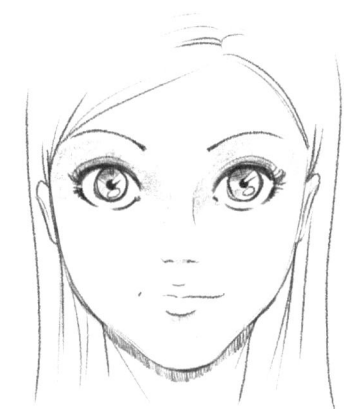

The hair reflects the light and creates sharp areas of light and shadow.

To give the effect of black or brown hair, we will use several dark tones, and we will accentuate the shadow with black.

For fair hair, we will use grey. On clothes, light and shadow are less sharp and alternate with gradual shades.

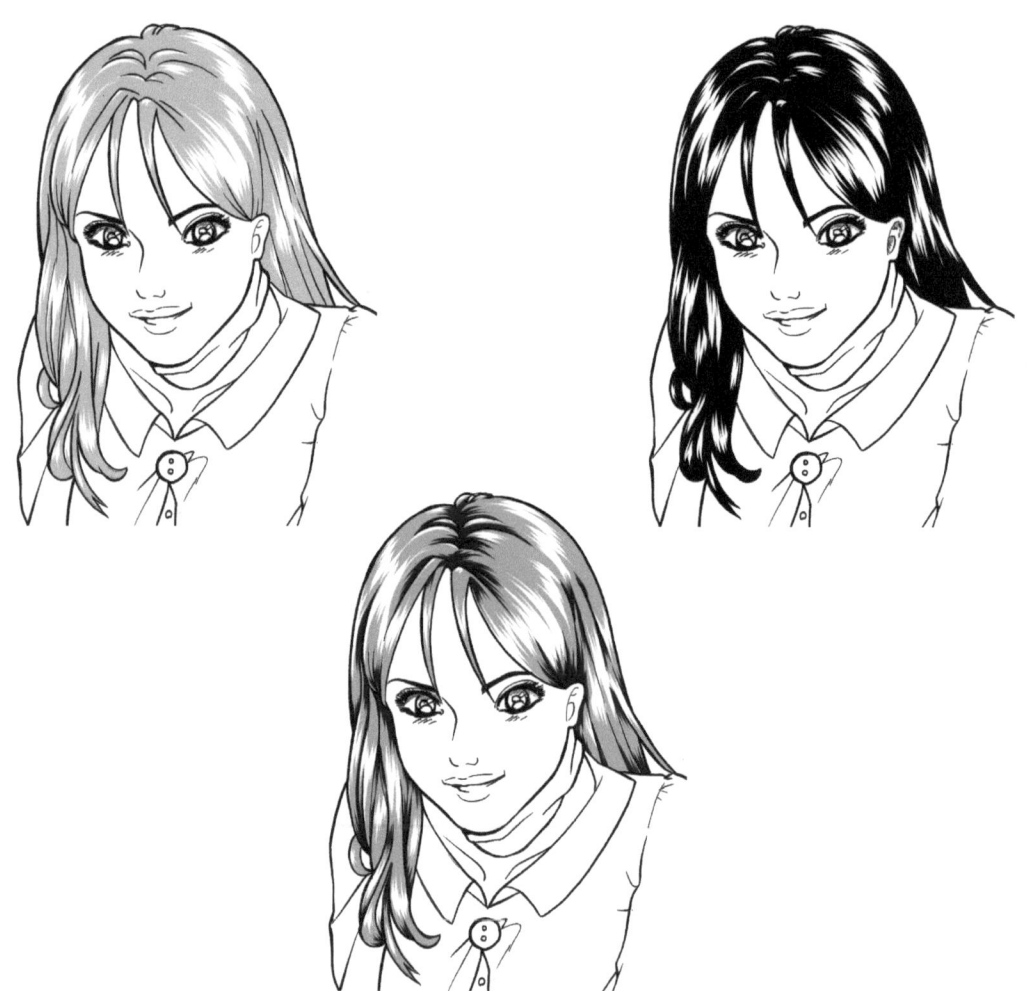

The point of light is the object's area directly hit by the light's source, and you should apply the shadow's rules to it because also the light determines the shape. The light's intensity and shade depend on: the type of surface, the proximity, or distance between the light's source and the object.

Place **the light sources** wherever you want inside the drawing. Sometimes a particular light gives particular suggestions.

The light can come from a candle, a lamp, a window, or if you have set the drawing outside, the light will be more diffuse and natural, and the source will be the sun.

We will simplify the study of shadows by dividing the image into 3 zones, as in the example: **the shadows, point lights, and the middle tone**, which is in the middle.

Define the areas and decide how to fill them and how to shade shadows and point lights. The image below has a predominantly frontal diffuse light.

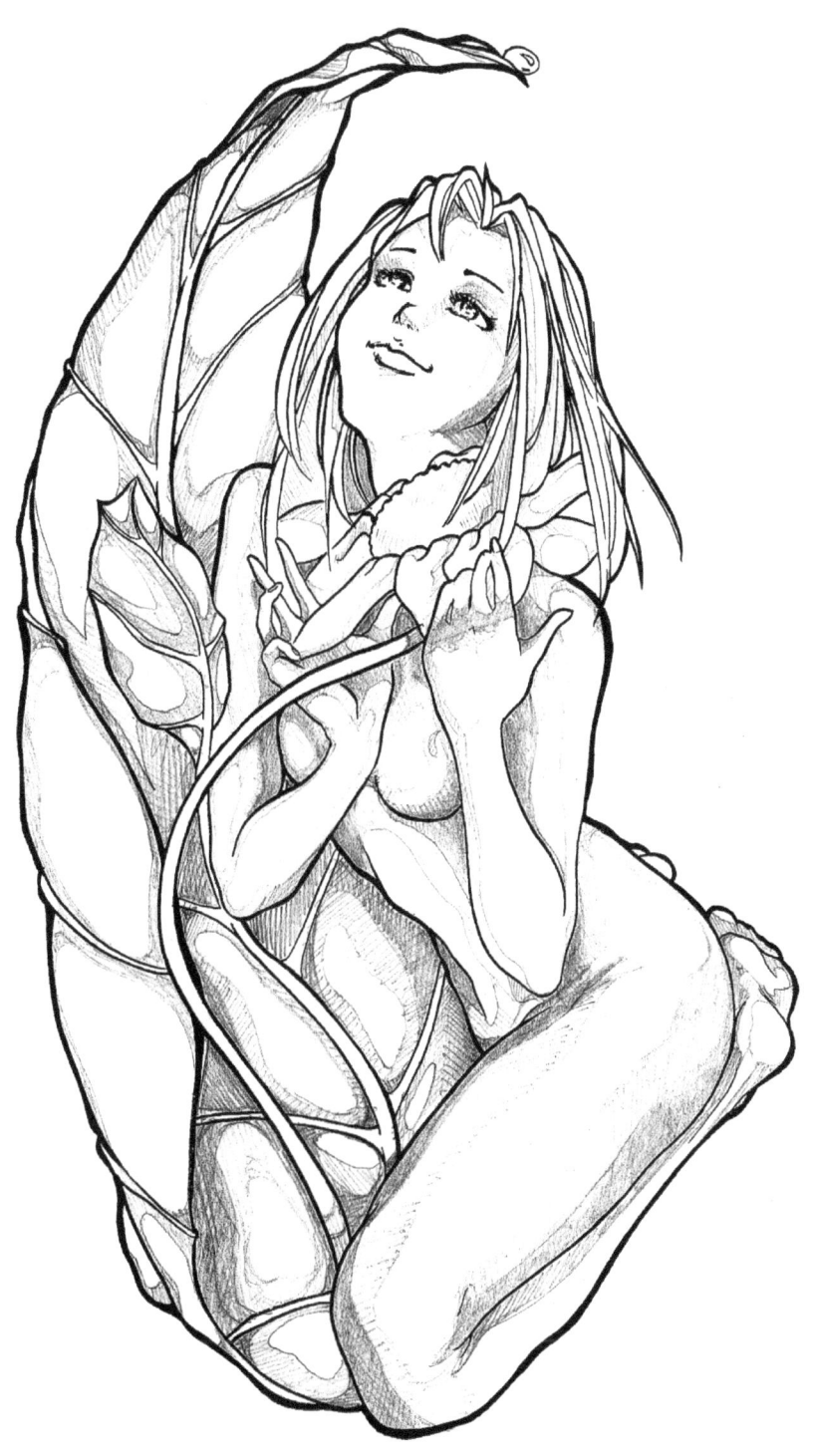

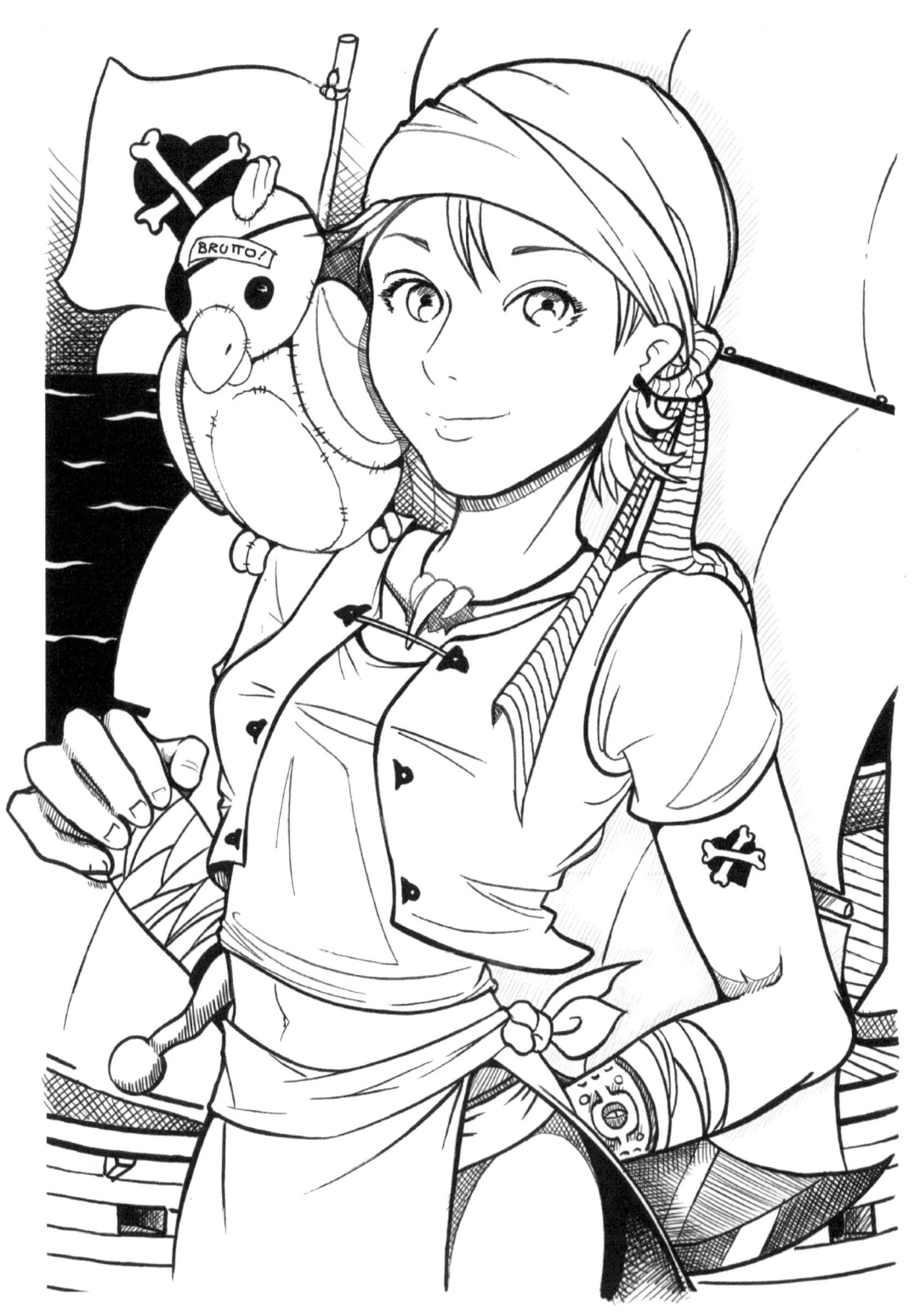

2. Fillings

2.1 Chiaroscuro

Fillings are the various ways to create the light-shadow effect and give three-dimensionality to a drawing.

Such as the **chiaroscuro** (1), the **stippling** (2) and **solarisation** (3).

In the **chiaroscuro**, the artist fills the shadowy areas with black. You can obtain greys and shades with hatchings or other effects.

The chiaroscuro is an essential technique. Combined with others, such as halftoning, gives effective results.

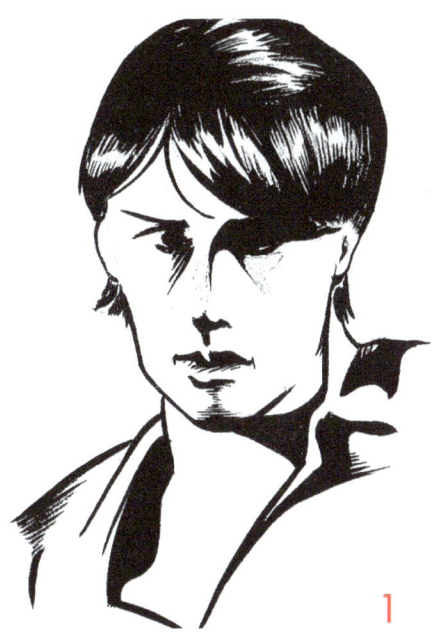

Use the **stippling** for suggestive, particular situations that give a specific impression.
Stippling consists of a series of points with different densities depending on shadow or light make it up.

Solarisation is a kind of light-dark filling without middle tones and contours. The effect is that of an overexposed photograph but combined with techniques such as halftoning, it acquires greater usefulness.

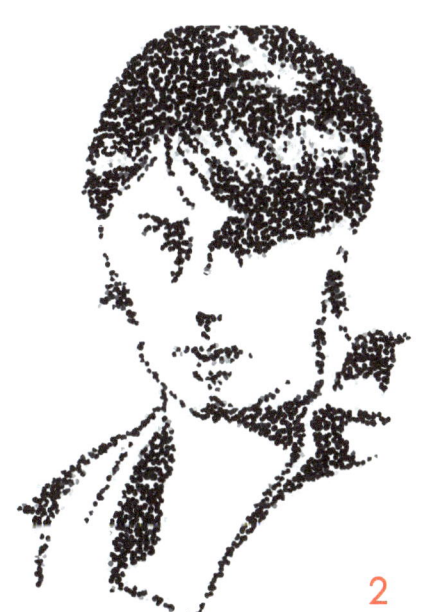

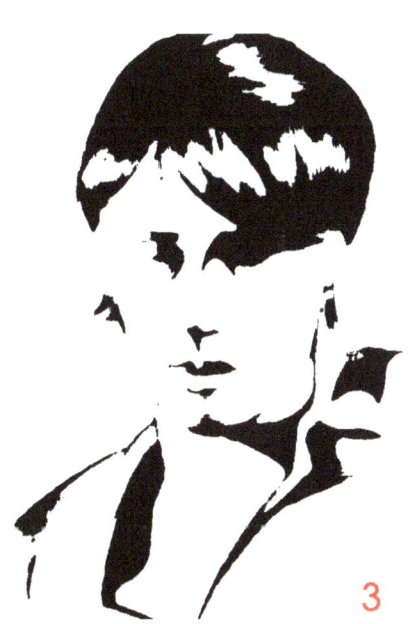

2.2 Hatching

Hatching is a technique used to create nuances between shadows and light points, with pencil or ink (pencil, nib, paintbrush, multiliner, pen).

It consists of making parallel lines, generally inclined and crossed.
Hatching consists of lines that have only one direction or be much more complicated with sections that have many directions and, therefore, create many intersections.

The lines that make up the shade follow two coexisting logics:
- The lines can start wide and then get thinner.
- There are crosses of lines in the dark part and fewer lines in the light part.

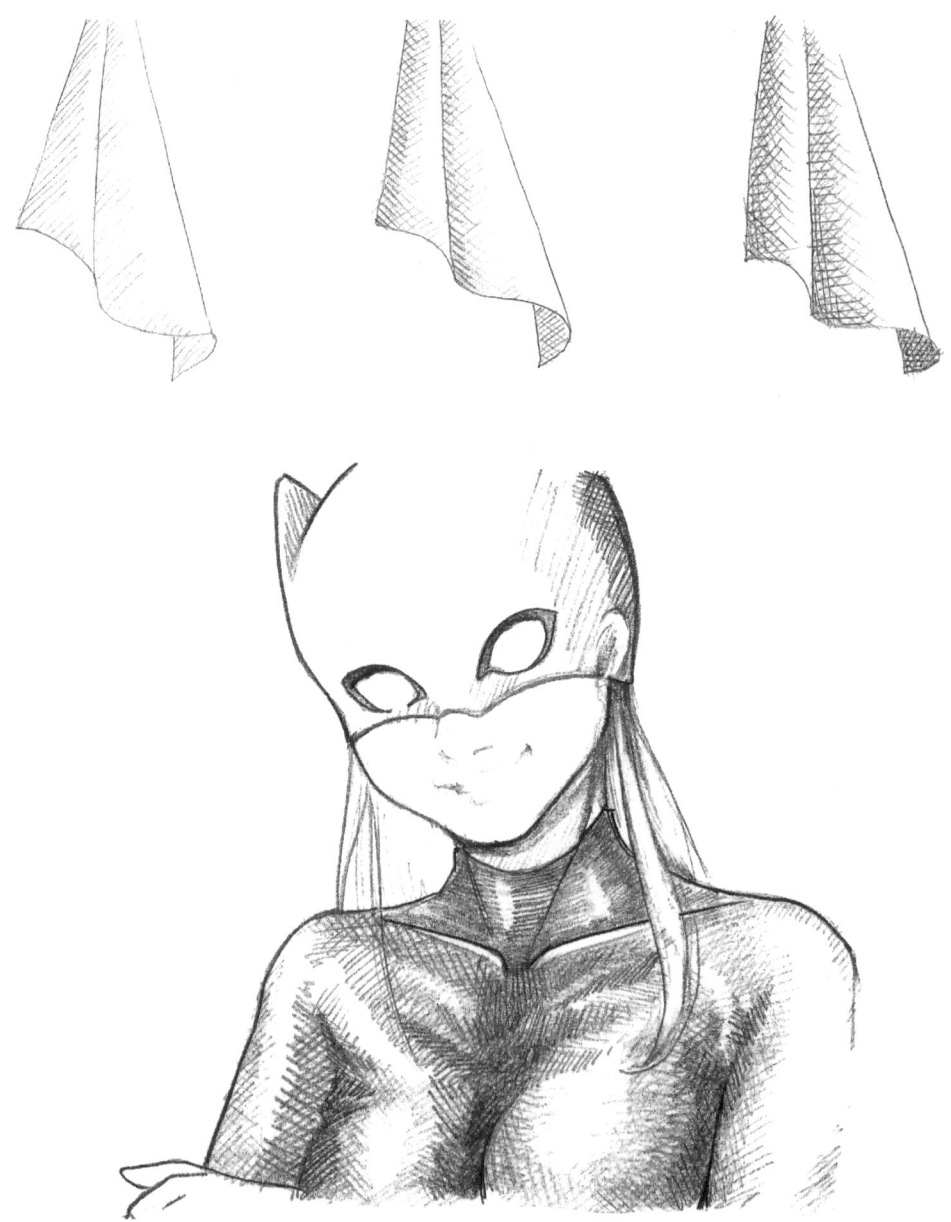

If desired, the hatching lines can curve following the surface on which they lie. This style will give more three-dimensionality to the drawing.

The best way to learn how to use hatching is to do a shadow study and practice, copying real figures if you need help.

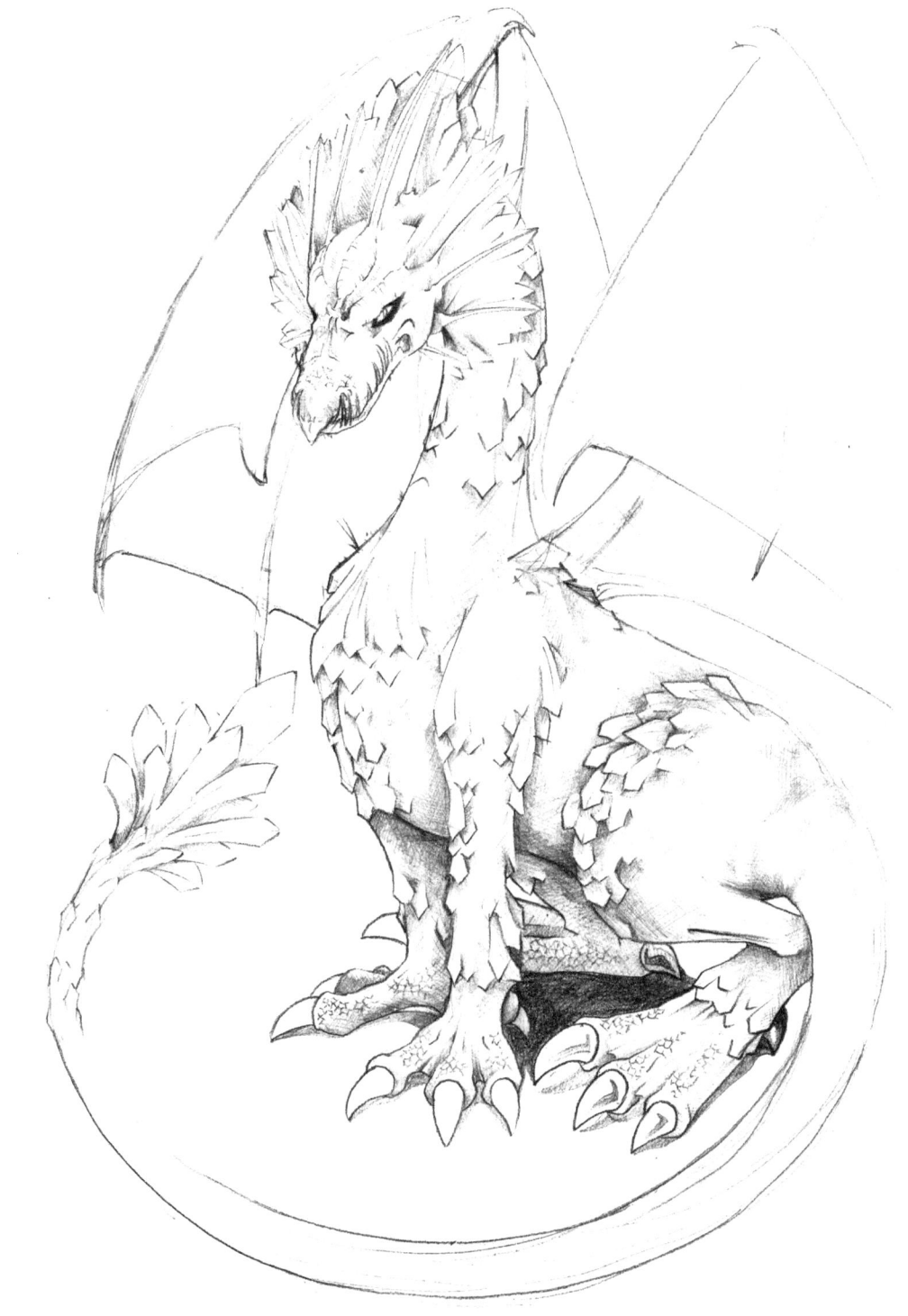

Hatching with ink

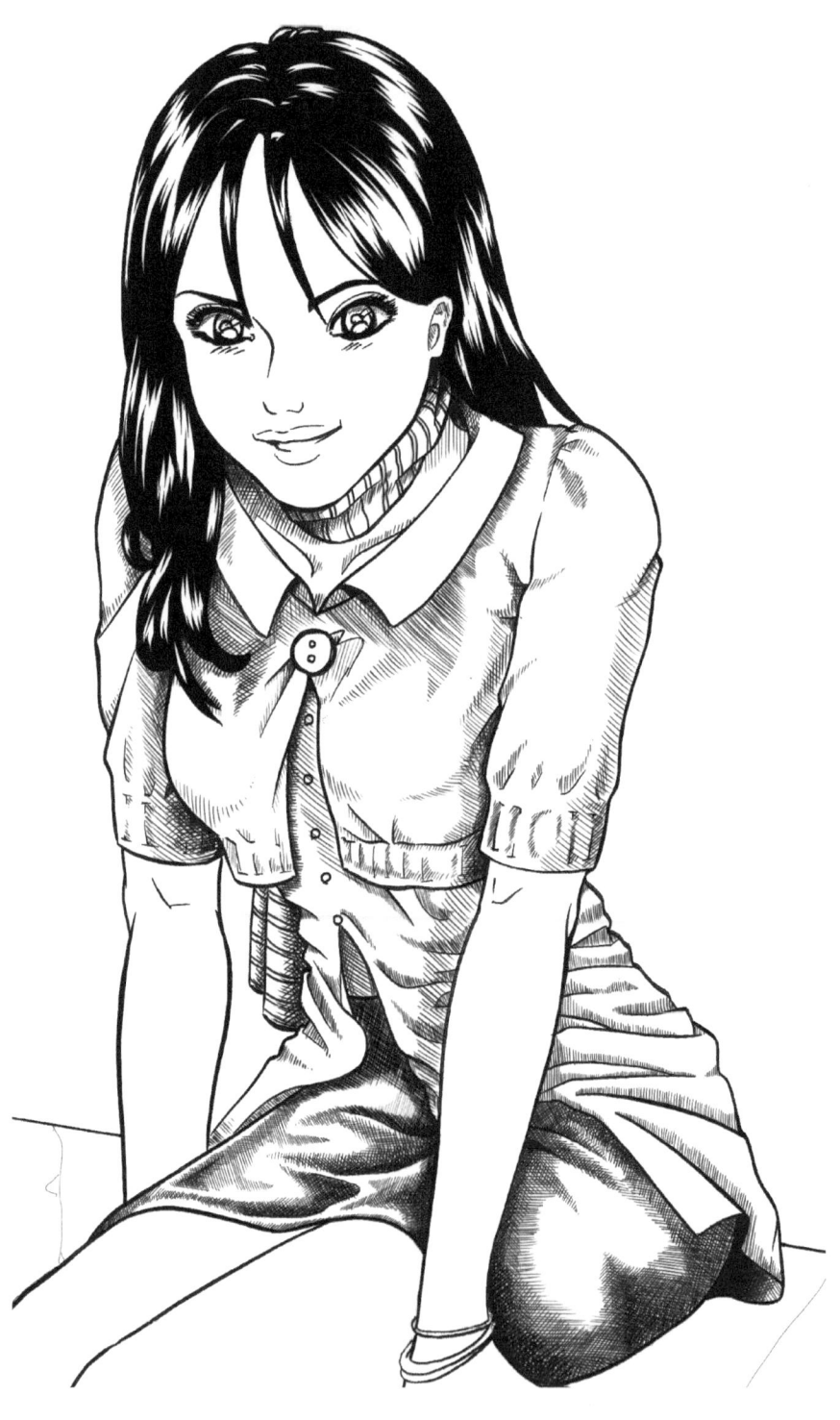

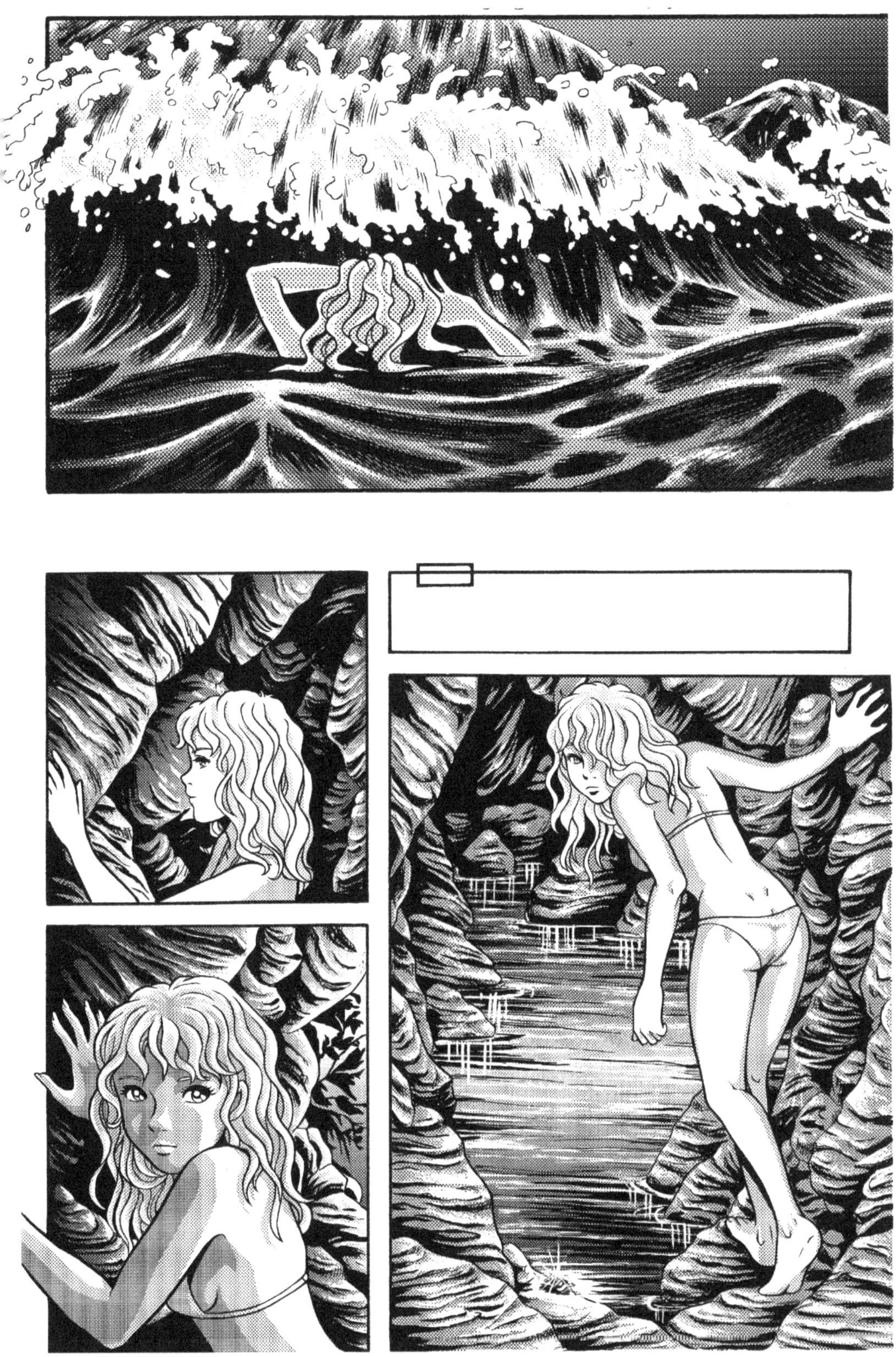

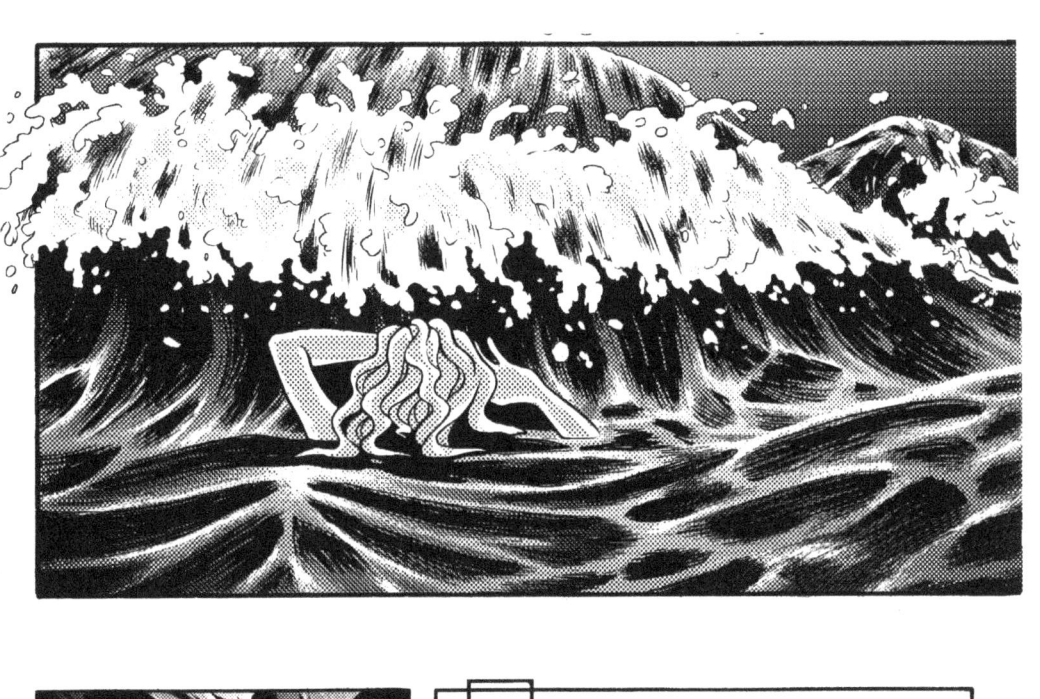

From **"Il Mare di Seira"**, drawing by Novella, inking and filling by Annarita Rimini.

2.3 Halftoning

This technique, typical of Manga, allows replacing the hatching with blurred chiaroscuro, consisting of dots, lines, or textures. The halftone screen is an adhesive sheet on which various motifs printed (it comes in tons of different types).

How to apply the halftone screen:

Apply different kinds of halftone screens onto the relative areas of the drawing. They reproduce shades of grey, from the lightest to the darkest tone. Choose halftone screens according to shaded areas and aiming to differentiate materials.

After cutting out a sufficient portion, place the adhesive sheet on the drawing.

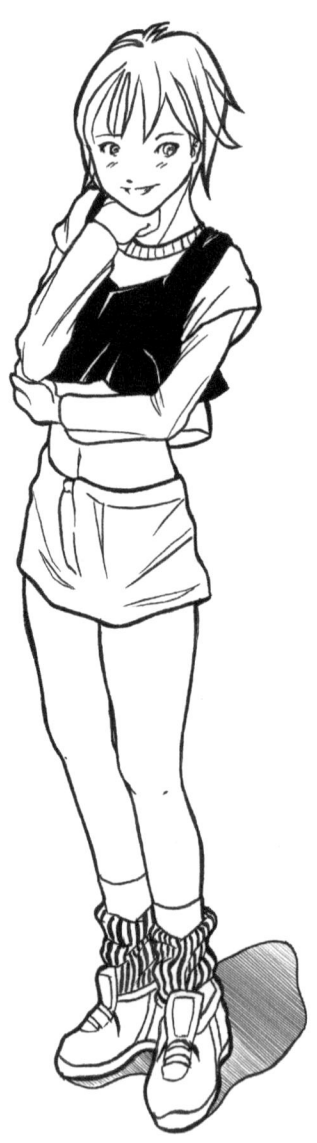

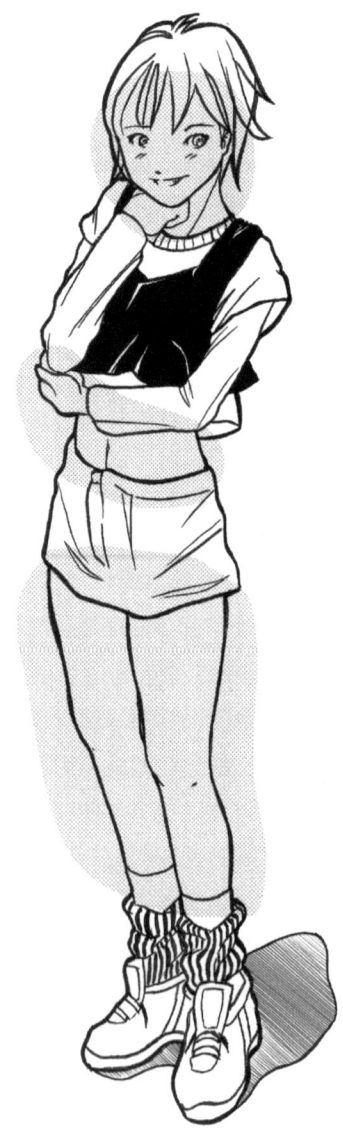

With the cutter, trim off the excess part, following the outline (white line), and remove it, taking care not to spoil the inking. Then press the halftone screen on the sheet to secure it.

Proceed in the same way with the other halftone screens. Then arrange them to add light and shadow effects. The cutter's ceramic tip is handy to create light points using it as a pen.

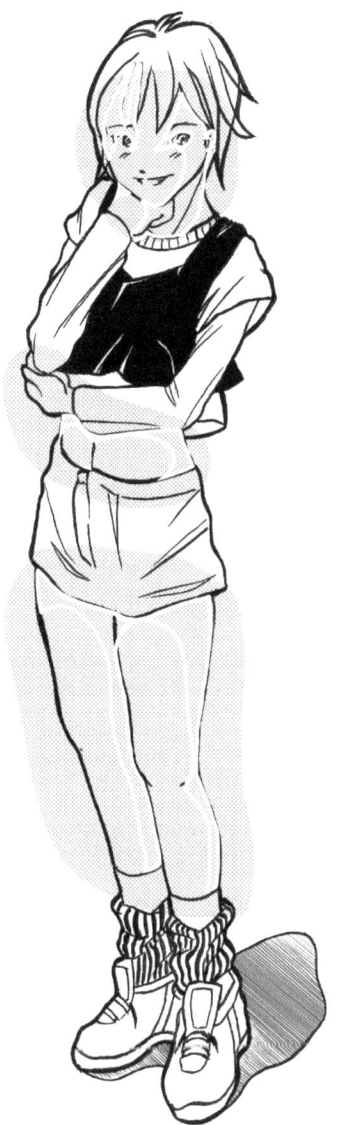
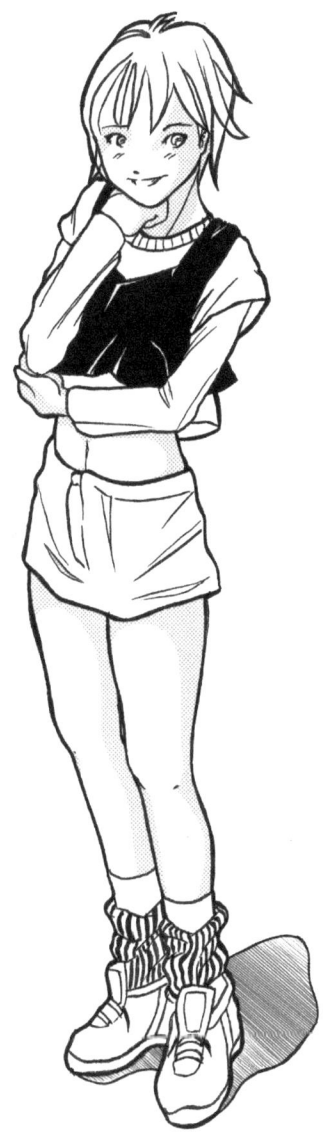

Processing halftone screens:

Once applied the halftone screens, they can be further processed using mixed techniques to make light and shadow effects.

Before applying effects, make sure that the halftone screen is firmly attached: press on the sheet with an appropriate tool. Pay particular attention to the corners.

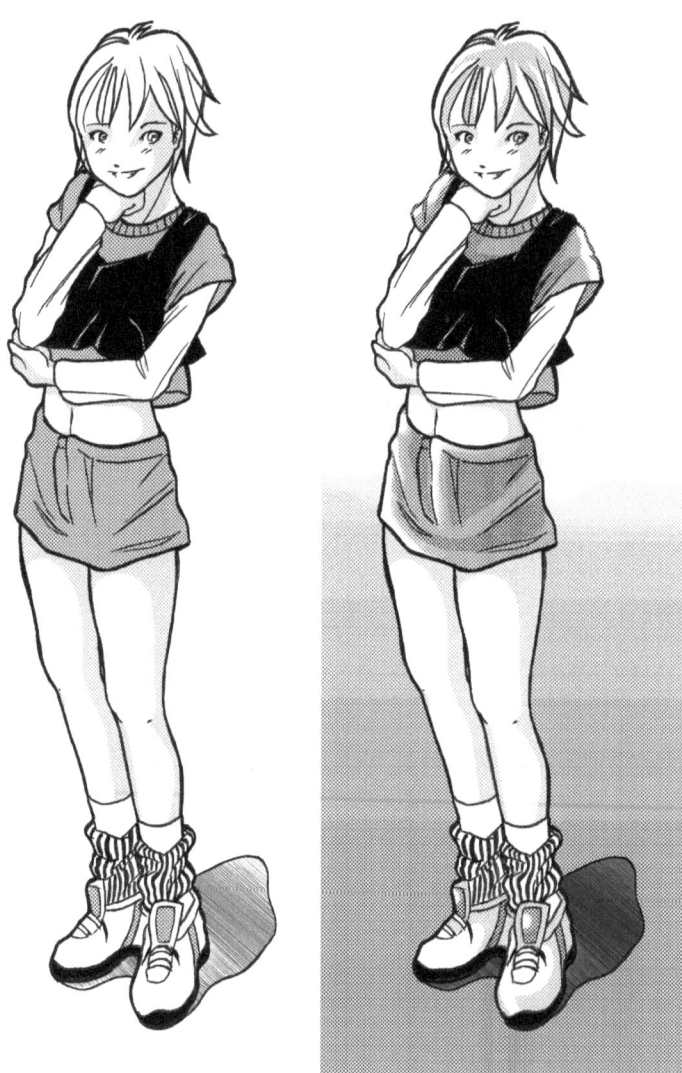

Techniques to obtain light points are: scratching the halftone screen with the cutter and create nuances, erasing some areas, or covering them with white paints (correction fluid, tempera, pens, and markers).

To create light on a dress (made of non-glossy material), fade the halftone screens by scratching them off in a delicate and precise way, as you would do drawing hatching.

To create this effect, use a standard cutter, a halftone screen's eraser, or a specific cutter with a thin ceramic tip.

Hairs are shiny surfaces, so to give light to them, we will use an intensely white, and we will not necessarily shade it. In this case, it will be possible to use tools for scratching the halftone screen, correction fluids, or white tempera to make an intense light.

Before using the halftone screens, fill the shady areas with black or hatching. However, this is not the only way to show shadows.

Keep in mind that shadows and lights depend on the scene's lighting, but they are also needed to detach the drawing levels.

In case one chooses to create the shading using the **overlapping of the halftone screens**, it is important to be careful. When overlapping them, try not to make a *moiré* pattern (it is a crisscross dots' plot).

We recommend using the same halftone screen already laid down to create the shadows. For particular textures, fill the shadows with black or hatching.

Use halftone screen erasers to create nuances on larger portions of the halftone screens, as happens in backgrounds.

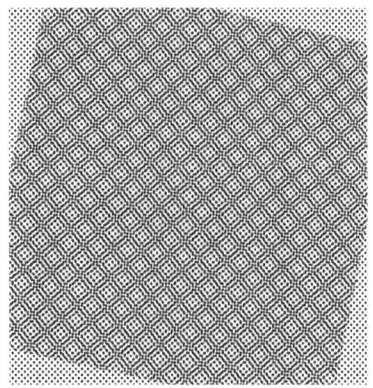

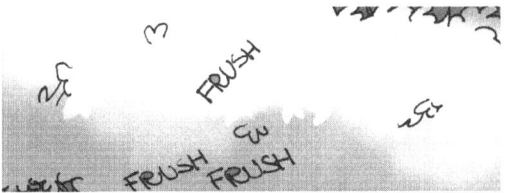

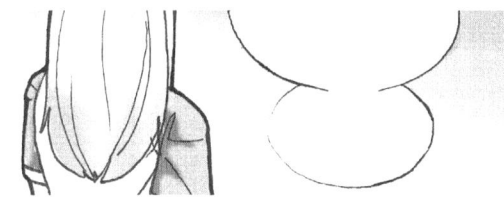

With the help of correction fluid, pens, markers, and everything that allows writing with white on a halftone screen, you can make various effects.

One of the simplest examples is to create small white dots around or onto the character to increase the richness of the drawing.

With white, it is also possible to draw illuminated hair against a halftone screened background and add details.

If a portion of the halftone screen has been cut or ruined, you can clean the area and, repositioning the pattern in the same direction, add the missing part (or the ripped part).

If a shade is not perfectly realized, is possible to shift it, cleaning the wrong part with white.

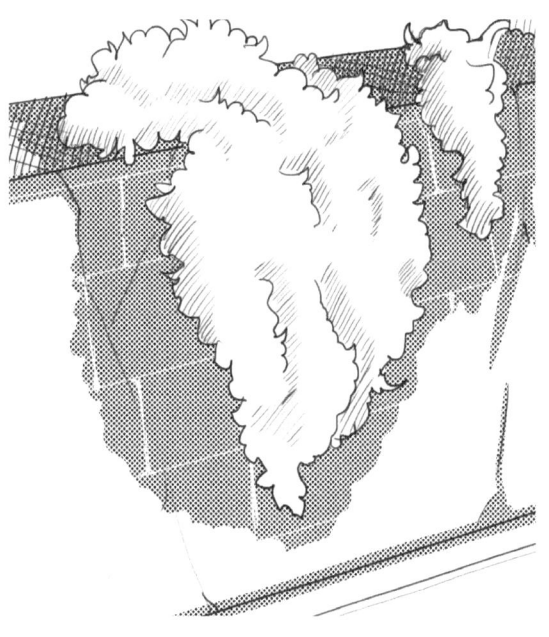

A great skill is to transform an error, perhaps irreversible, into an element of the drawing; this not only crucial for halftoning but for every production.

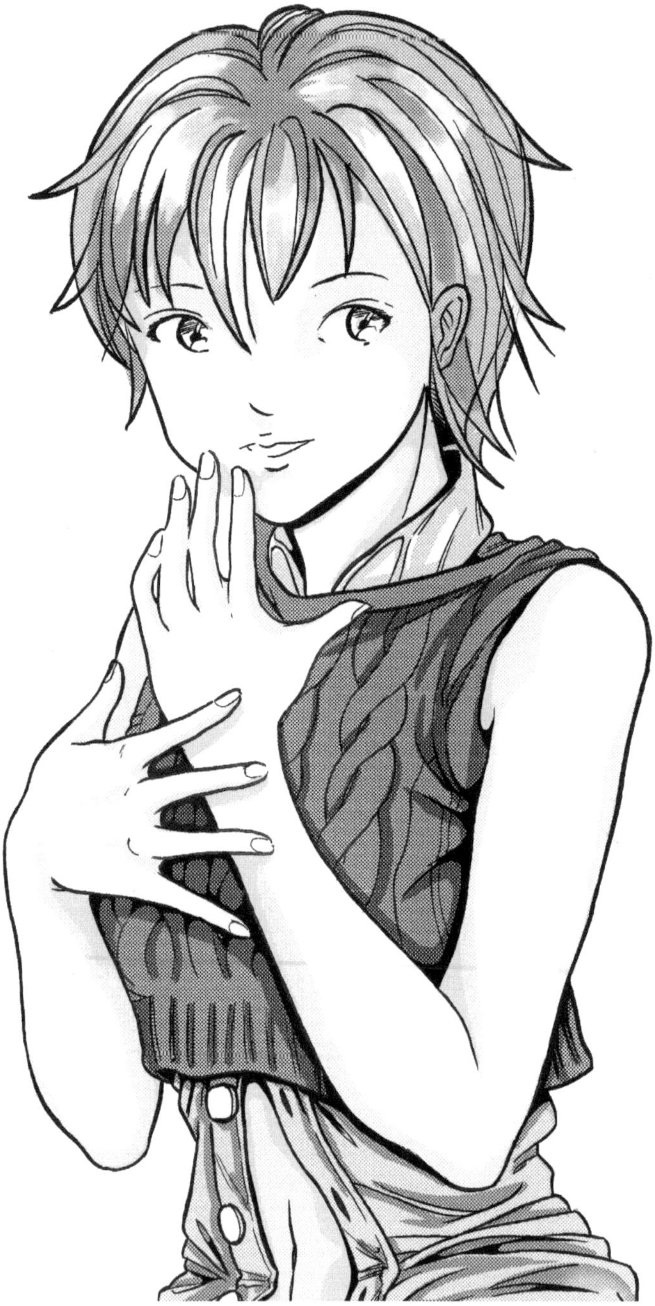

It is also possible to insert shadows after pulling the screens because the India ink and other inks can write on them.

Knowing how to **correct mistakes** is necessary. Even the best mangaka's hand can slip and cut out a needed part of the halftone screen. A mangaka could scratch it off too vigorously and tear it, or maybe to add unfilled shaded areas.

The adhesive screen application is a long and meticulous procedure, and experience is required to achieve good effects. However, Manga continues to offer halftone screened panel pages, the halftone screens, indeed, can also be **digital** and this method has supplanted manual processing, which covers about 10% of production.

As for many techniques, it is practical to start from the non-digital procedure and practice until you master it. Only then, it is possible to switch to digital, taking advantage of all the tools available that risk to be misused without a previous analog experience.

Digital halftoning on the side

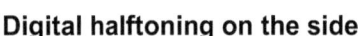

There are many varieties of textures: ready-made backgrounds, trees, landscapes, or abstract decorations and shapes. The speed of digital is much faster than *handmade*, but this one still makes works more valuable.

Manual halftoning

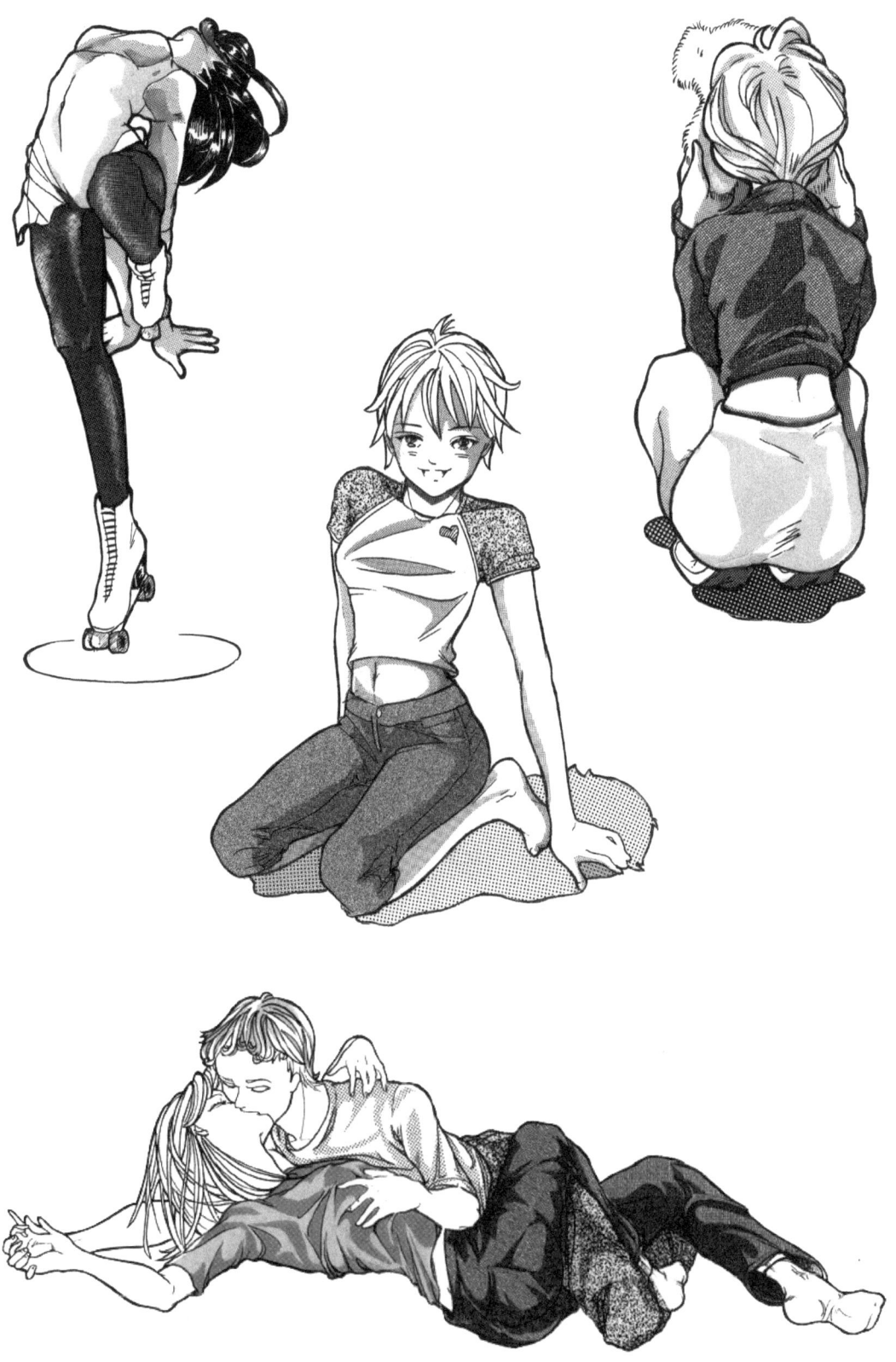

2.4 Filling effects

It is possible to use effects produced by tools such as **sponges**, **brushes**, and **masks** to enrich a drawing.

Dip the **sponges** into the India ink, loading the right amount of ink and use them by dabbing the ink. Of course, the sponge texture can change and be wide or dense, depending on the type of decoration you decide to use.
You could use the **brush** by swiping a finger to splash the color on the paper. Try this tech-

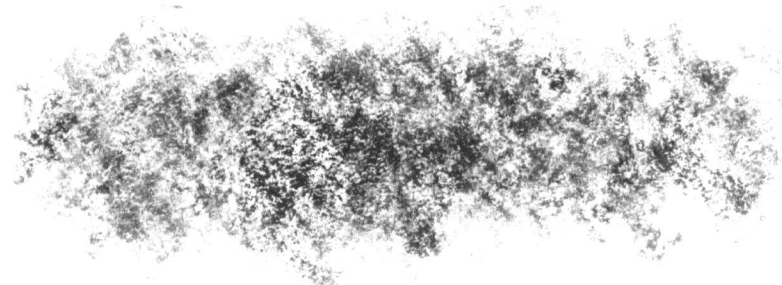

nique several times to understand how to achieve the desired effect: the closer you are, the bigger the dots will be and vice versa. It is a very coarse airbrush effect.

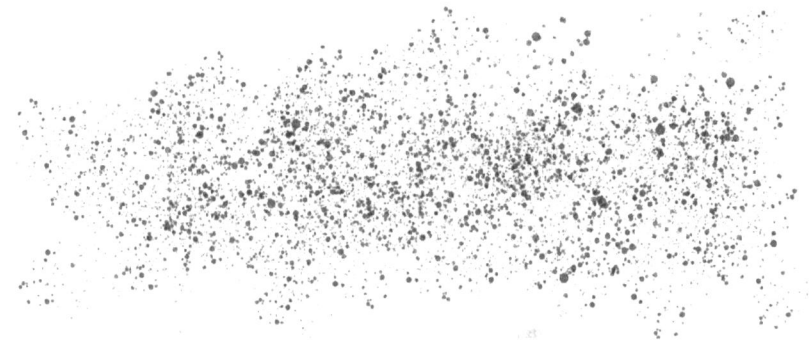

Sponge and brush can be associated with **masks**. Masks allow working by isolating unfilled parts of the drawing.

The masks have holes of various shapes, and it is also possible to make them yourself.

You can choose from adhesive sheets to cut or liquid masks to distribute by the paintbrush and easily remove these tools with an eraser.

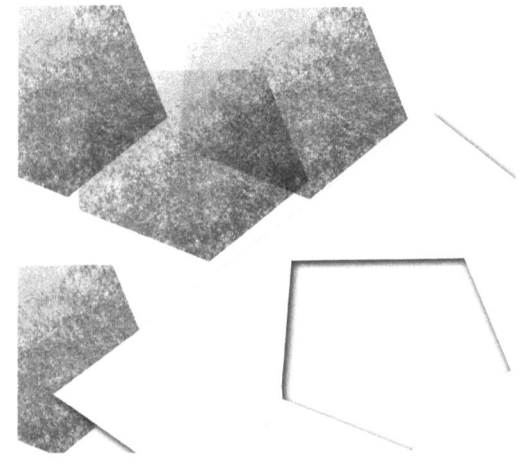

Sponges   **Masks and Stencils**

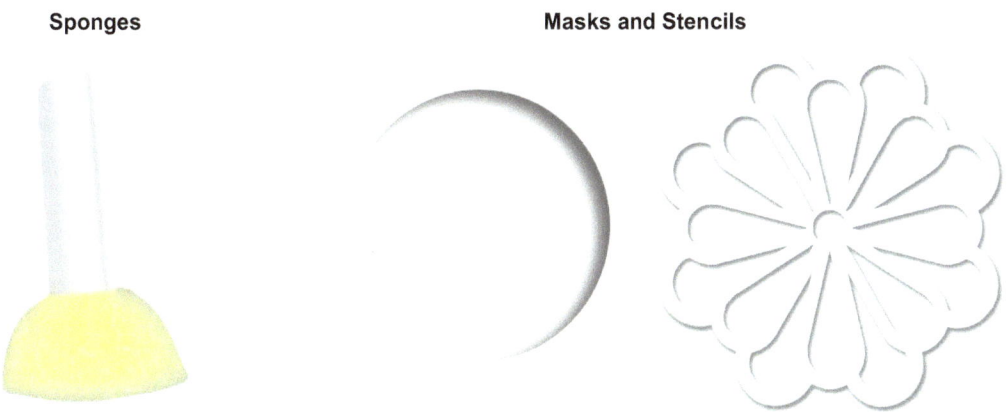

We talk about this technique because, in Manga, it is often used for backgrounds or as decoration, especially in shōjo. Start by overlapping the mask on the drawing, and then dab the sponge into India ink or color. Gradually dabbing the sponge makes it possible to create shades both inside the mask and outside the shape (see images below).

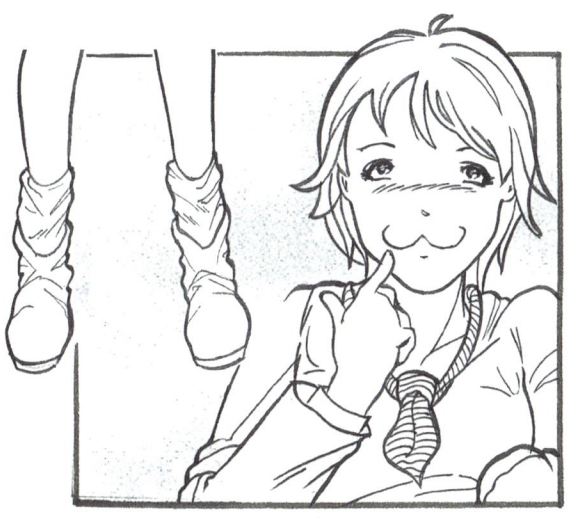
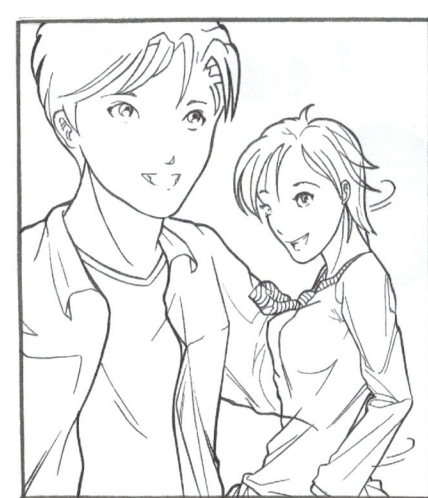

Halftoning and sponging effects

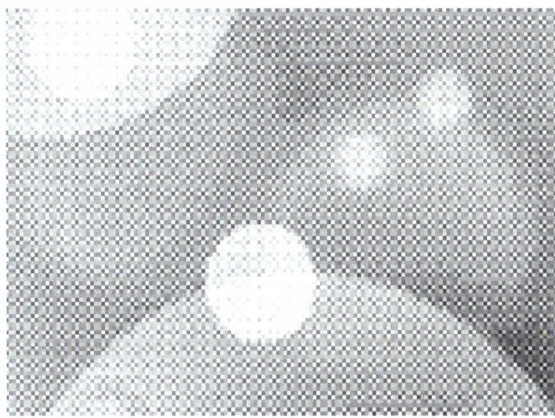
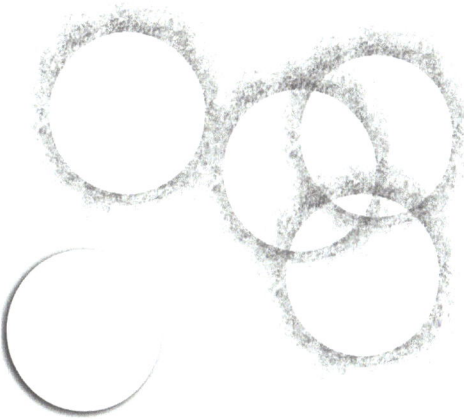

2.5 Coloring: the Pantone

To deal with the coloring topic, it is necessary to mention the techniques used in the Manga. The coloring of Japanese drawings is generally light, delicate, and prefers pencils, watercolors, and non-covering techniques often mixed.

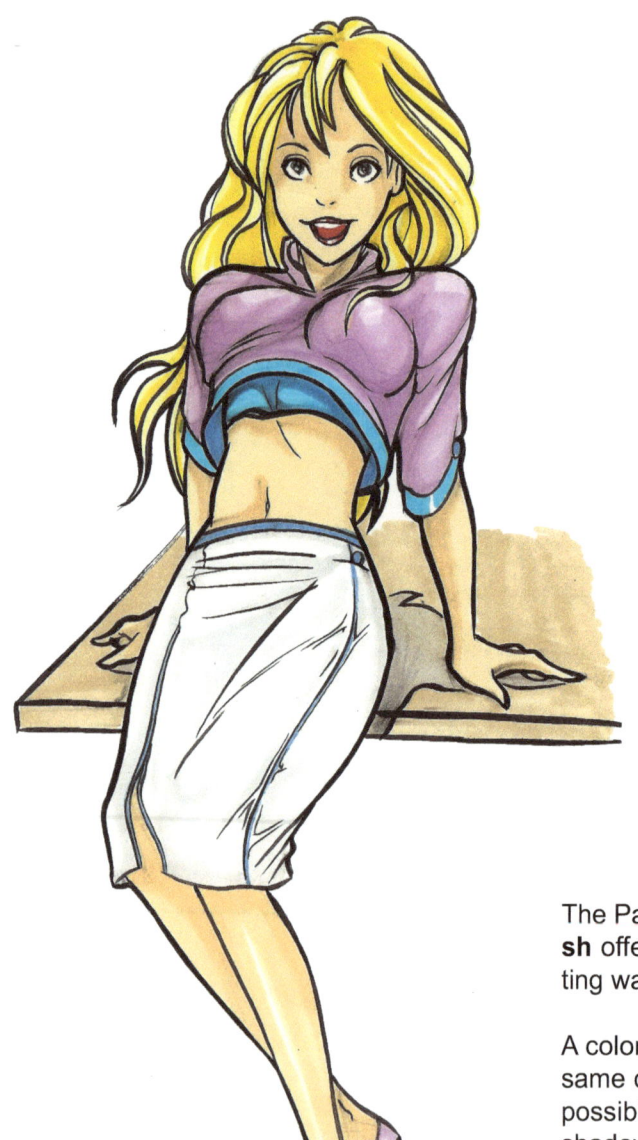

Talking about coloring, in general, is not very explicative, so we chose one of the best-known techniques to explain the subject in depth.

The **Pantone** is a marker pen capable of distributing color evenly.

You can make backgrounds without stains and apply uniform shades thanks to the solution contained in the Pantone.

It is an ink that spreads and mixes very easily without leaving streaks and marks.

The Pantone has various tips: **super-brush** offers complex effects, almost simulating watercolor effects.

A colored area will darken if we apply the same color over it several times. It is also possible to create nuances, shades, or a shadow zone.

You could achieve nuances made of 1, 2, or 3 colors (having a primary color in common).

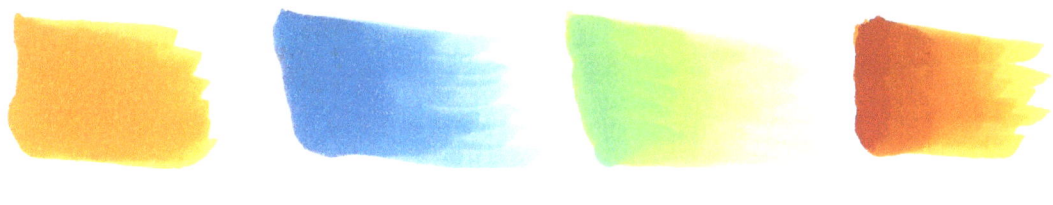

| homogeneous coloring | shading in 1 tone | shading in 2 tones | shading in 3 tones |

How to make nuances:

It is necessary to know about the use of **brush tip** (super-brush) and about the fact that **ink spreads**, to understand the techniques that express the full potential of Pantone.

Use Pantone as a paintbrush, thanks to its tip. The tip creates a wide or small stroke, depending on the **pressure** applied by the hand. The first step is to learn how to create lines that start wide and then become narrow.

The second concept, related to ink, is that by making a line **quickly**, it will be possible to notice a reduction in color in the final part (it will fade).

The combined effect of **pressure and speed** will generate the "brushstrokes" of gradient color. The color's tendency to conform will complete the effect.

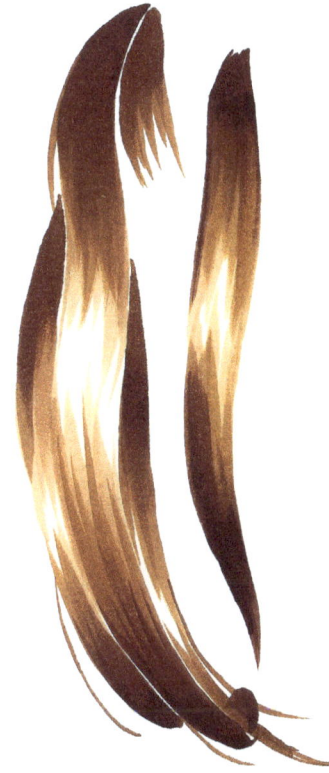

Another technique to create a nuance between two colors is to let different Pantones' tips to touch each other. The light one will absorb the darker color. At this point, coloring a small area, the released color will naturally fade from the darker to the lighter one.

When the "brushstroke" technique (pressure/speed) will be acquired, it will produce a very impressive coloring.

It is a functional technique for hair (see image) and for areas that need to appear shiny. In this case, it is sufficient to leave the illuminated area blank.

The technique is the same for shading colors, but one color should shade towards the other. Otherwise, it will create unerasable steaks.

It is crucial, before coloring a drawing, to study the shadows. Then will be easy to know where the light points and the shadows are.

The colors must be at least 3 for each section of the drawing: **a base, a medium tone, and a shading color**. Apart from gleaming surfaces, all other spaces need a warm or cold base for the light points.

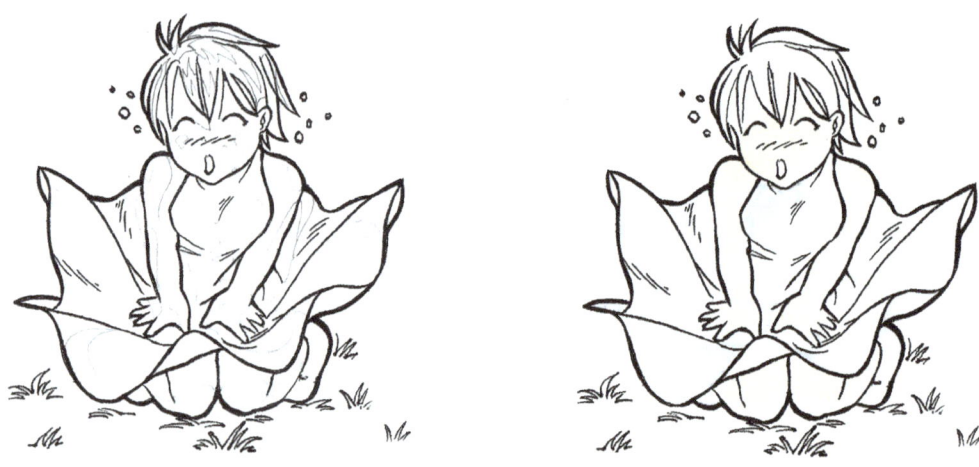

The **base** is an extremely light, almost invisible, color. It creates a warm effect on yellow tones and a cold effect on the blue tone. Choose the base according to the color of the medium tone or according to the global light's effect. The **medium tone** is the color of the objects; to give depth to the subject, add shadows with a **darker color**.

The contrast between the three sections can be sharp or blurred to give more depth to a drawing.

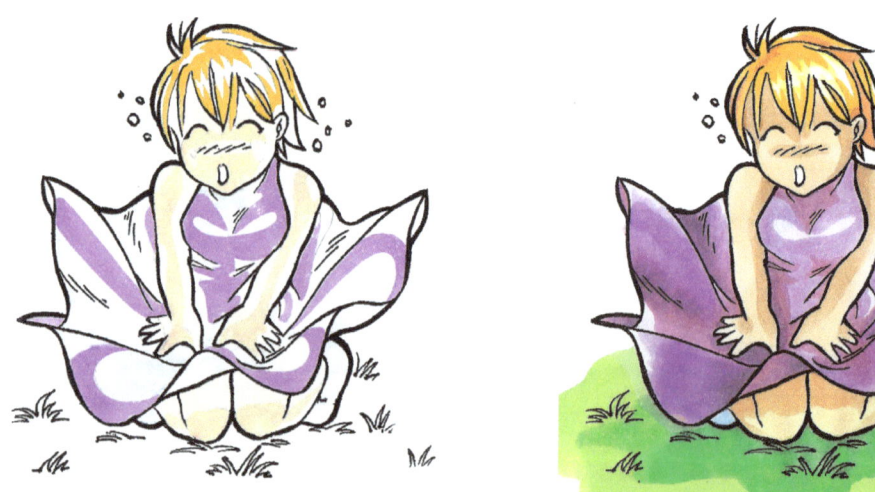

ssional result using this technique correctly.

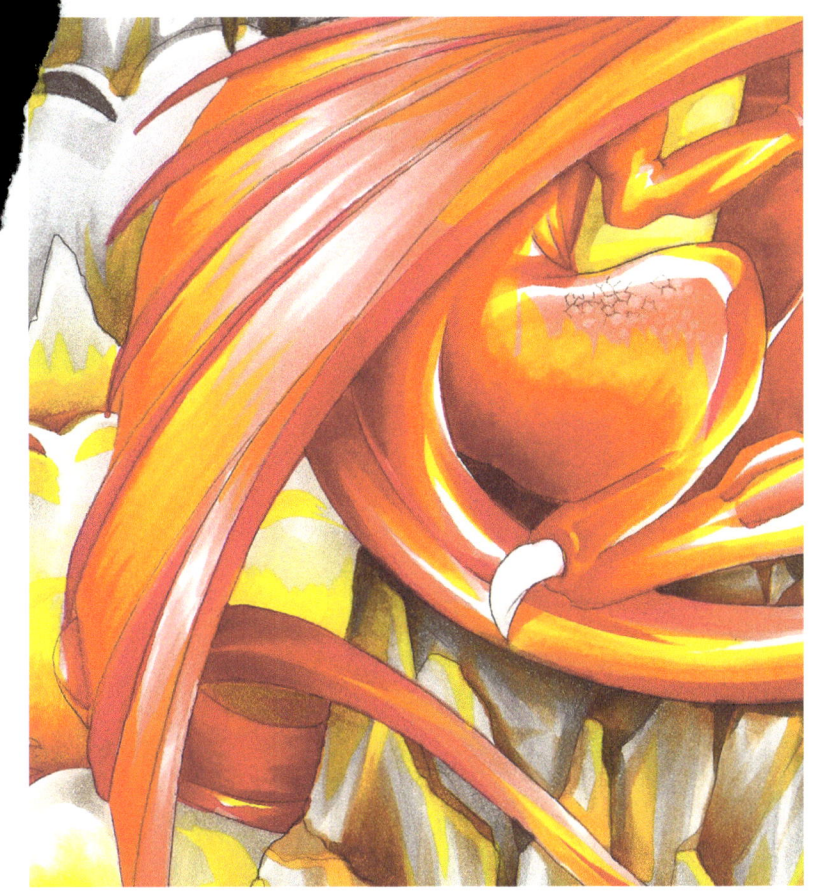

Always keep in mind that the ink spreads out, depending on the kind of paper, to prevent the color from passing over the edge of the drawing when coloring close to a margin.

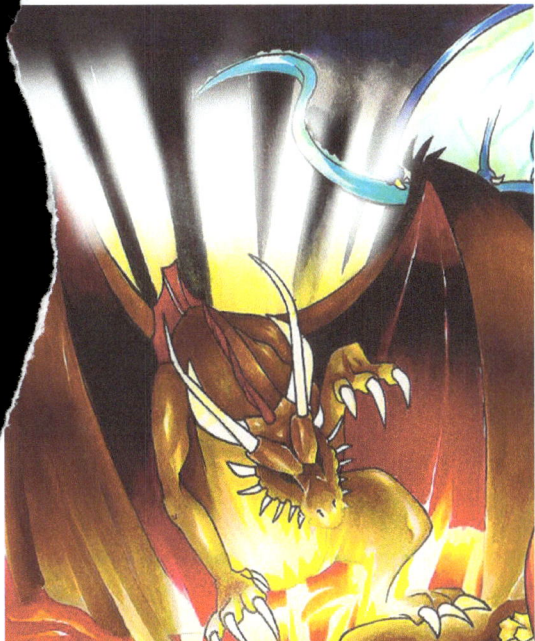

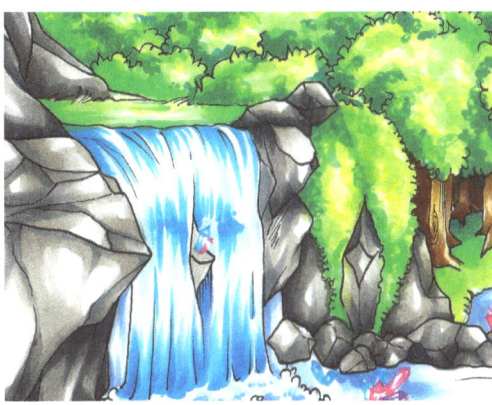

The last step is the **choice of colors**. Do the coloring matching upstre[am] method is to create a **palette** and modify it until the chosen colors create a [ef]fect.

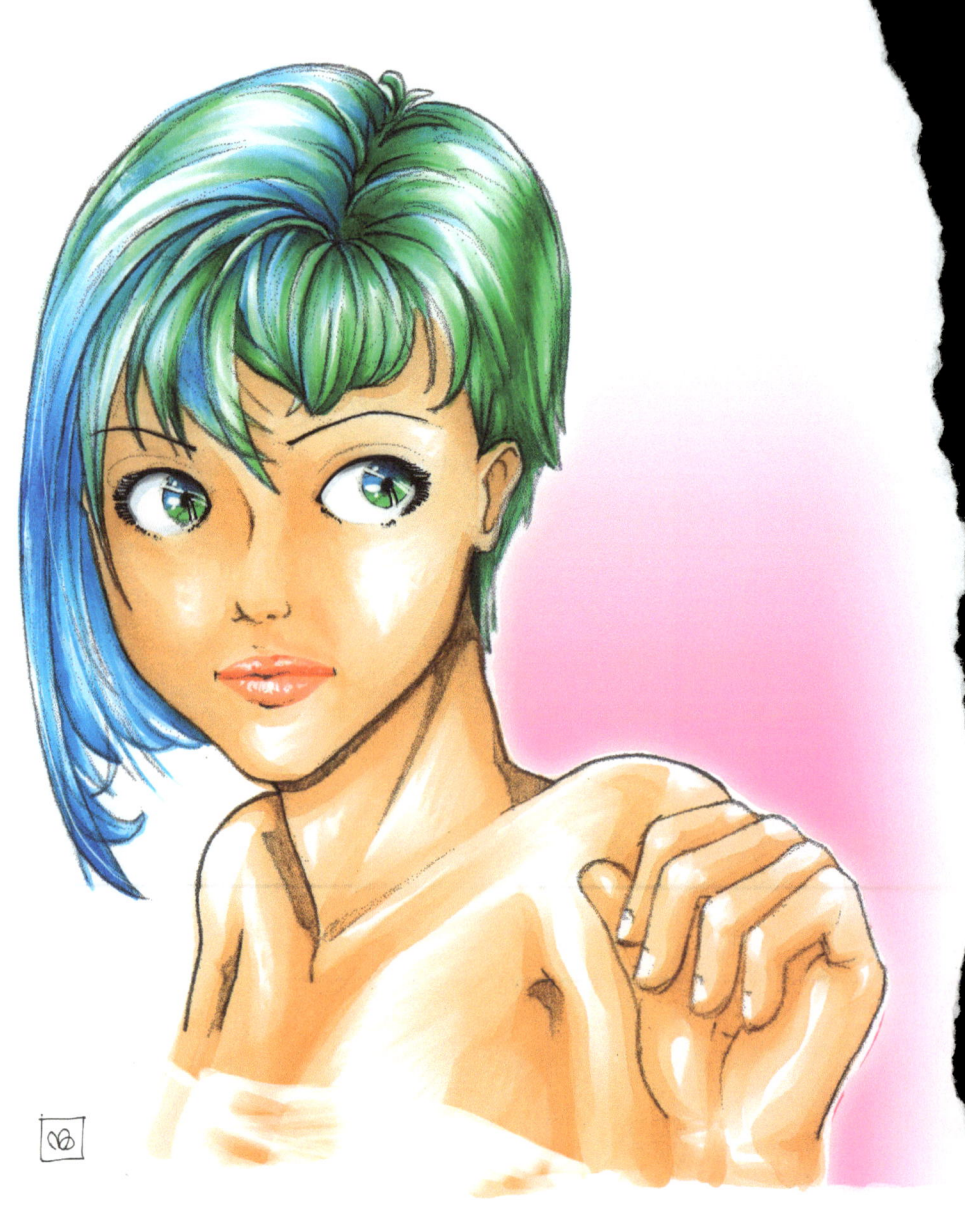

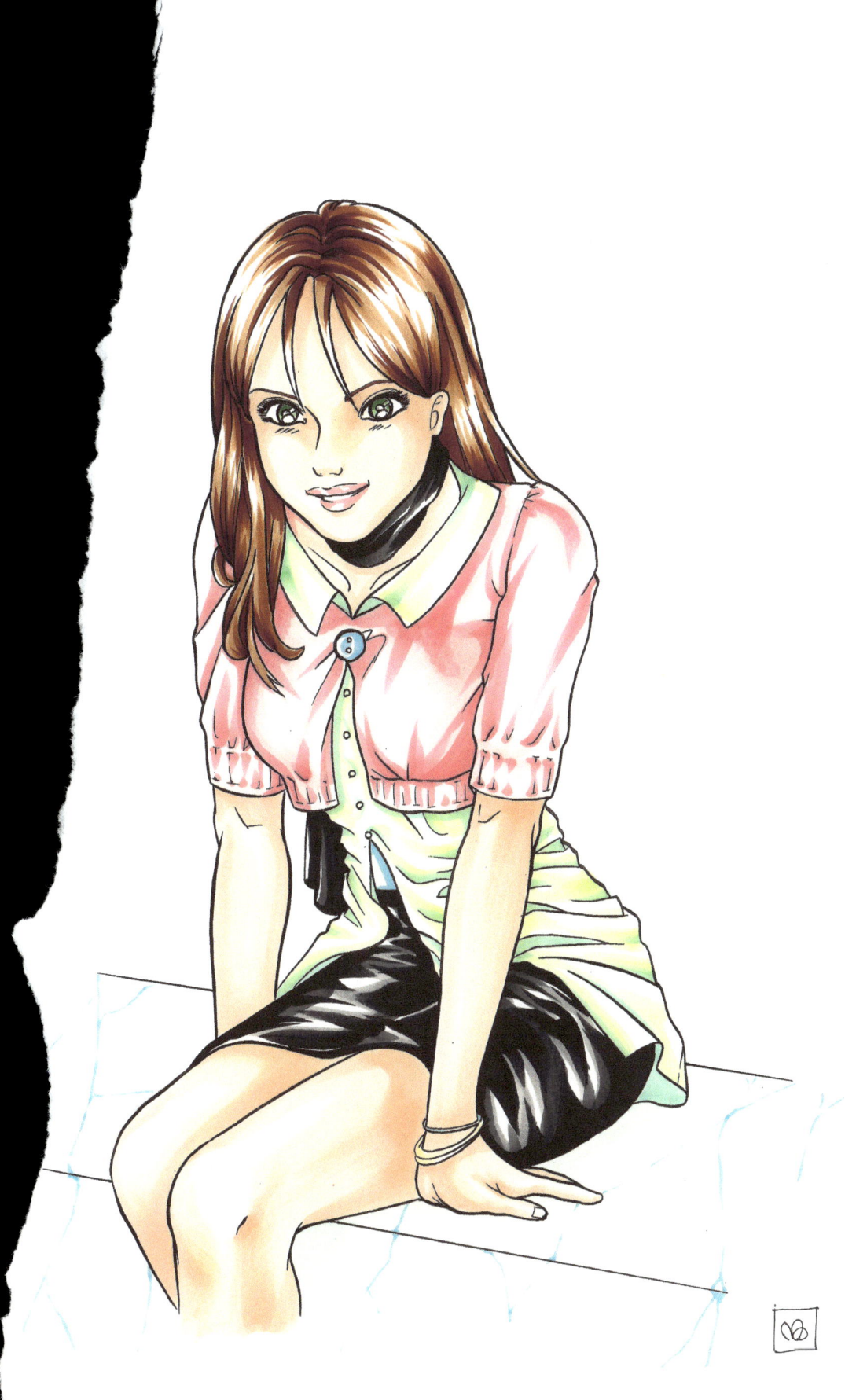

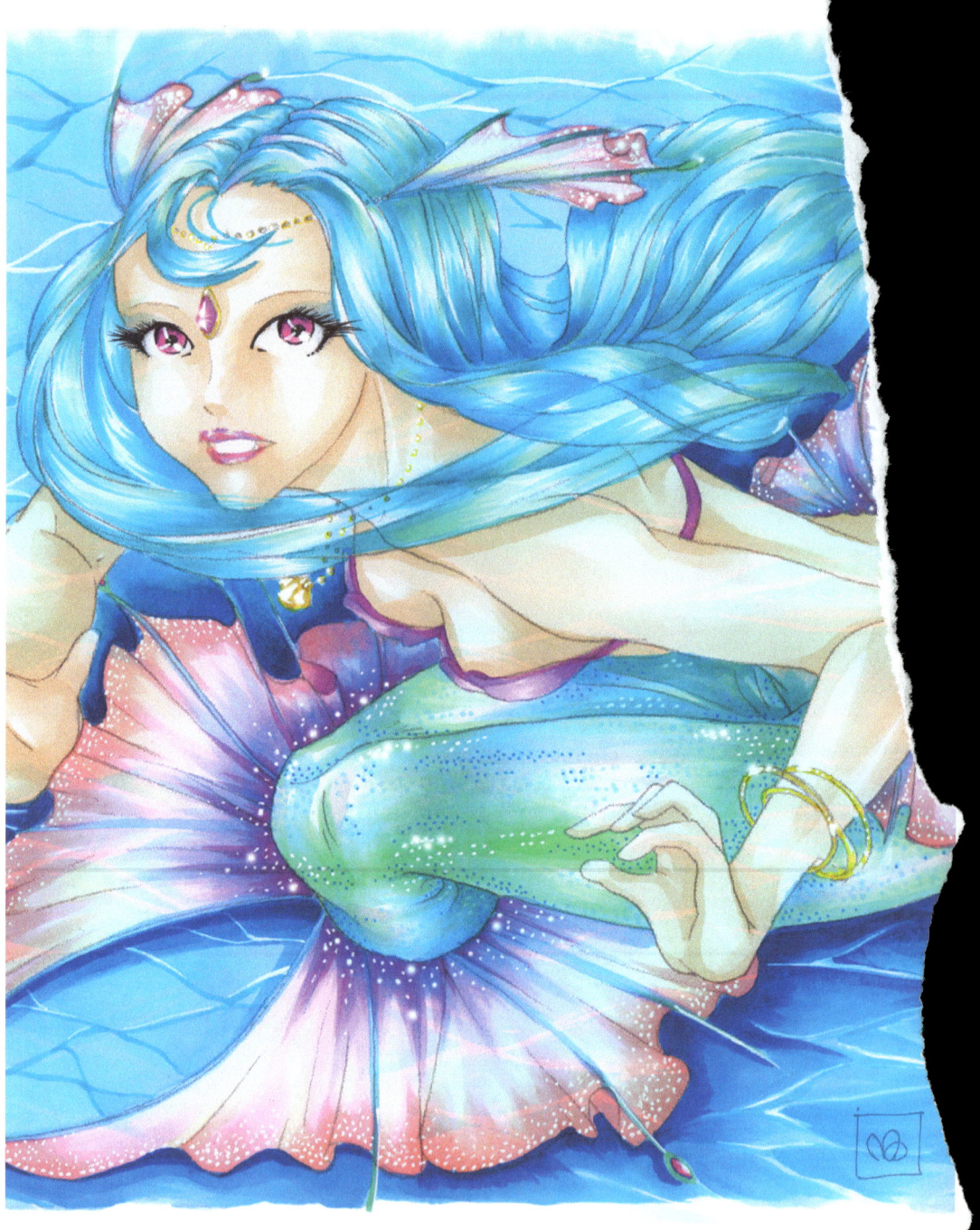

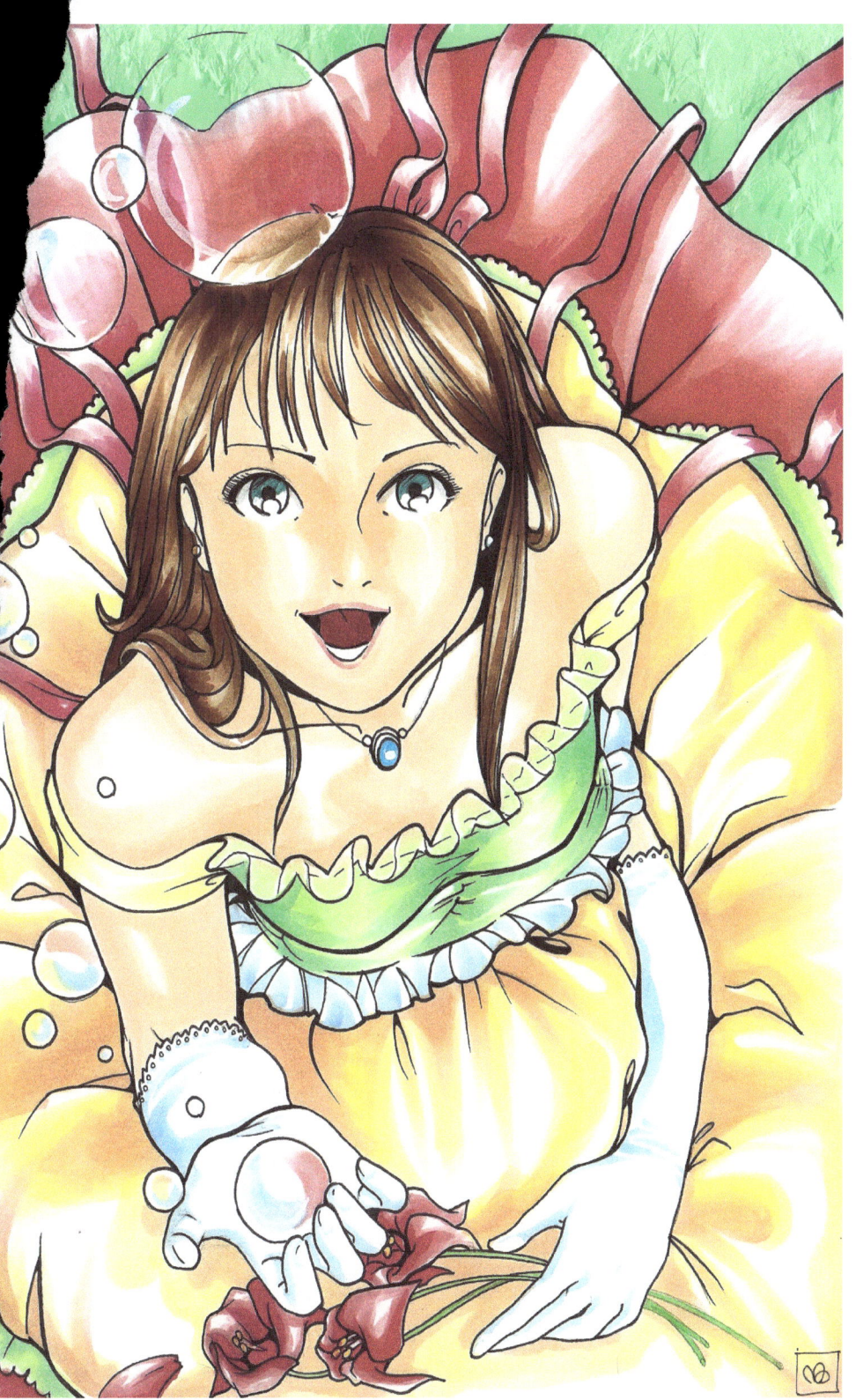

...r books of Manga's series "Techniques Manual with Novella Manga Artist's style".
...plete artistic path for designer and cartoonist.

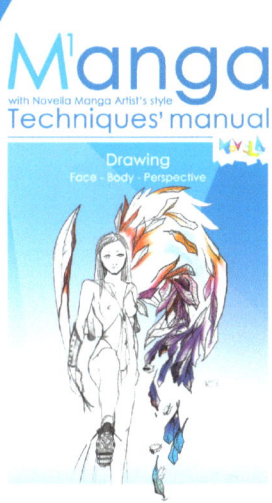

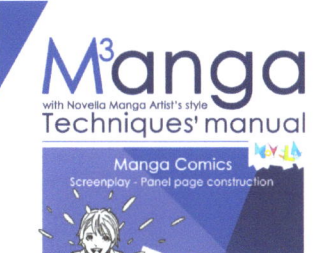
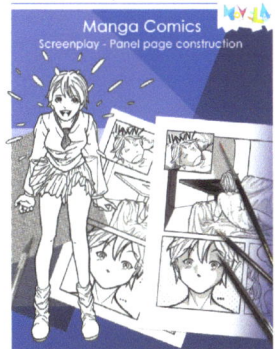

FIRST SECTION, LEARN TO DRAW

First section materials

1. **Introduction to drawing**
   Drawing
   Differences between Realistic, American, Comics and Manga
   Introduction to Manga drawing

2. **Drawing fundamentals**
   Volumes' three-dimensionality
   The perspective
   Manga proportions
   Eyes
   Face elements
   The face
   Drawing different ages
   Face Perspective
   Hairstyles
   Expressions

   The Body
   Body volumes and manga proportions
   The male body
   The female body
   Body volumes in perspective

3. **Hands and feet**
   The hand
   The foot

4. **The deformed style**

5. **The harmony of movement**

6. **Drapery: drawing clothes**

THIRD SECTION, COMICS

Third section materials

1. **Manga, the Japanese comics**
   Introduction to comics

2. **Formats**
   Strips
   Panel pages

3. **Panel pages elements**
   Panels and scenes
   Speech balloons and lettering

4. **Screenplay and narration**
   Creating a subject
   Screenplay: choice of scenes
   Narrative techniques

5. **Panel page construction**

6. **Cover's study**
   The cover
   Marketing mentions

7. **Terminology**
   Technical Glossary
   Abbreviations of screenplay's shots

GEM Design

GRAPHIC & MANGA ACADEMY

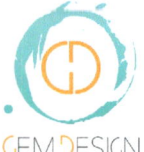 The manual was created by collecting the techniques proposed in the school's courses. After years of teaching and experience in transferring notions, we elaborated and simplified the methods for learning manga drawing according to the artist's style.

Follow NOVELLA MANGA ARTIST

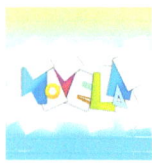 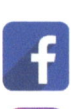

For informations and contacts:

www.facebook.com/novellamanga

www.instagram.com/novellamanga

Text:
G&M Design, copywriting

Technique:
Novella Bardelli, artist and teacher

Drawings:
Novella Bardelli, artist and teacher

Layout:
G&M Design, graphics

Marketing:
Alex Gambini, social media marketing

Translation:
Silvia Coppola, translator

Text's editing:
Silvia Coppola, editing

All graphic productions and texts (with the exception of the third section materials' photos, Glossary and Terminology which present contents copyright-free) in the manual are original and owned by G&M Design. Their distribution, reproduction, use for unauthorized commercial products, application of unauthorized logos and other non-legal uses are forbidden.

www.ingramcontent.com/pod-product-compliance
Lightning Source LLC
Chambersburg PA
CBHW040414220526
45473CB00004B/1241